Praise for *The Mind-Body Method*

'An essential how-to book to reduce stress, calm anxiety and keep your brain active'

Nir Eyal, international bestselling author of *Hooked* and *Indistractable*

'The relationship between the mind and the body is one of the most important questions in science, and Dr Hansen explores this in a lucid, fascinating and inspiring way'

Johann Hari, bestselling author of *Stolen Focus, Lost Connections* and *Chasing the Scream*

'Dr Hansen's *The Mind-Body Method* is an ultimately practical guide to regaining a sense of peace in a world that seems to be coming undone'

Dr Russell Kennedy, physician, neuroscientist and author of *The Anxiety Prescription*

T0322113

Praise for *The Happiness Cure*

'Kidneys evolve. Lungs evolve. As do brains, and in ways relevant to our pursuit of happiness and our vulnerabilities to mental illness. In *The Happiness Cure*, psychiatrist Anders Hansen explains how our brains have evolved more slowly in these realms than has our lifestyle, and the malaise that this mismatch produces. This wonderful book is steeped in insights, clear explanations and empathy. Most of all, it imparts deep wisdom about how we should live our lives.'

Robert Sapolsky, Professor of Biology and Neurology at Stanford University, and *New York Times* bestselling author

'A brilliantly researched book that will transform how you think about happiness.'

Thomas Erikson, international bestselling author of *Surrounded by Idiots*

'Anders Hansen's work is the antidote to our modern-day struggles.'

Dr Rangan Chatterjee, bestselling author and creator of the podcast *Feel Better, Live More*

'A fascinating exploration of the ways in which our ancient neurologic wiring is mismatched for the modern ecosystem. By understanding depression and anxiety through the lens of evolution, we can make sense of the growing despair in the world today and do something about it. This is a must-read for anyone hoping to understand the human brain.'

Dr Anna Lembke, *New York Times* bestselling author of *Dopamine Nation*

'By describing our minds as the products of evolution, Hansen shows invaluable new ways for understanding and living with our most important mental ups and downs. *The Happiness Cure* uses direct and accessible language to present the exciting promise of a scientifically informed psychiatry.'

Richard Wrangham, author of *The Goodness Paradox*

'Anders Hansen is a highly regarded scientific communicator who, in this book, seeks the keys to our well-being through human evolution. It is both an encouraging and a comforting message which describes how our brains are wired for survival, rather than constant well-being.'

Thomas Perlmann, Professor of Molecular Developmental Biology at Karolinska Institute, Sweden

'The market is flooded with books on how to achieve good mental health, including everything from meditation and mindfulness to treatment with SSRI medication. But the brain is not developed for our well-being, but rather for our survival and reproduction. Stress states, panic disorders, obsessive-compulsive disorders and even ADHD and autism spectrum diagnoses have evolutionary benefits. The psychiatrist Anders Hansen has understood this and delivers his thoughts in his new ingenious and well-written book. It's a must-read!'

Hugo Lagercrantz, Professor Emeritus of Paediatrics at Karolinska Institute, Sweden

the
ADHD
advantage

OTHER BOOKS BY ANDERS HANSEN

The Happiness Cure (2023)

The Attention Fix (2023)

The Mind-Body Method (2024)

the
ADHD
advantage

Why Your Brain
Being Wired Differently
is Your Superpower

Dr Anders Hansen

Vermilion
LONDON

Vermilion, an imprint of Ebury Publishing
20 Vauxhall Bridge Road
London SW1V 2SA

Vermilion is part of the Penguin Random House group of companies
whose addresses can be found at global.penguinrandomhouse.com

First published by Bonnier Fakta in 2017

This edition published by Vermilion in 2024

www.penguin.co.uk

A CIP catalogue record for this book is available from the British Library

ISBN 9781785044946

Typeset in 10.5/15.5 pt ITC Galliard Pro by Jouve (UK), Milton Keynes
Printed and bound in Great Britain by Clays Ltd, Elcograf S.p.A.

The authorised representative in the EEA is Penguin Random House Ireland,
Morrison Chambers, 32 Nassau Street, Dublin D02 YH68

Penguin Random House is committed to a sustainable future
for our business, our readers and our planet. This book is made
from Forest Stewardship Council® certified paper.

Dedicated to

Hans-Åke Hansen (1940–2011)
Vanja Hansen and Björn Hansen

There are more and more discoveries of people that have something that could be called a defect and yet have immense talents in one way or another.

ANTONIO DAMASIO

CONTENTS

PREFACE

ADHD IS NOT A made-up diagnosis. If there is one thing you should take from this book, that's precisely it. Attention deficit hyperactivity disorder (ADHD) is a set of innate personality traits that historically may have conferred such significant advantages upon us humans that we might owe our very existence to them. These traits likely played a role in humans leaving Africa and colonising the entire globe. But it's not just in the past that ADHD has brought advantages; it can still confer significant benefits today.

In this book, I will demonstrate that ADHD can present you with a unique toolbox, if you only know how to use it. That being said, I do not in any way wish to trivialise the challenges of ADHD – you would be deluded if you imagined that having ADHD is a walk in the park. The challenges cannot be ignored.

As a psychiatrist, my job is to assist people with problems stemming from various psychiatric conditions. So why do I think it's important to discuss the advantages of ADHD? Well, the first 15–20 years of a person's life are incredibly formative, especially when it comes to self-perception. ADHD is rarely a good fit with modern society, especially school. Those who perform worse than their peers, when they are compared to others for the first time in their life, often feel stupid and worthless. In my work, I have seen far too many examples of low self-esteem having lifelong consequences, and I want to change that.

Harnessing the advantages that ADHD can offer requires hard work. The first step is knowledge: to learn what ADHD actually is and how one can actively work on putting it to good use. That's precisely what you'll be doing in this book. This is not a textbook that covers every conceivable aspect of ADHD – such a book would be thousands of pages long. Instead, it's a popular science book that highlights one aspect of the most hotly debated condition of our time and how it can indeed serve as an advantage – if you know how to use it.

Anders Hansen

Chapter 1

TWO SIDES OF THE SAME COIN

SO WHAT IS ADHD really? Is it a disease? A disability? A super-power? Is it something the pharmaceutical companies have invented to sell medicine?

A Google search for 'ADHD' yields more than a billion hits and there appear to be as many opinions as there are posts online about our era's most vexed and debated medical diagnosis. Millions of people are diagnosed with ADHD each year – yet three decades ago, the diagnosis didn't even exist. In other words, it's easy to be left feeling both perplexed and dizzy by all the opinions, but I hope to bring some clarity.

Let's start from the beginning. For someone to be diagnosed with ADHD, they must face challenges in three areas: concentration, hyperactivity and impulsivity. The disadvantages of ADHD may include struggling with:

- maintaining concentration
- finishing tasks
- following instructions
- listening to others
- organising and planning
- sitting still; their legs may shake and they may fiddle with things – motor activity
- waiting one's turn
- being impatient
- staying calm; instead they are restless and always 'on', like an engine that's always running
- feeling constantly understimulated

Do you feel like this describes you or someone you know? If so, that's not surprising. We all have these traits to some extent and fall somewhere on the 'ADHD scale'. Some of us have a lot of these traits and are thus higher on the scale, like me. Others scarcely have them at all and will be lower on the scale. A small percentage have such pronounced traits – and, more importantly, experience such significant difficulties as a result of them – that it's justified to diagnose them with ADHD and administer treatment.

Take another look at the list. It's not surprising that everything on it presents challenges. For a psychiatric diagnosis to even be considered, the symptoms must cause problems. This doesn't mean that ADHD *only* causes problems, however. There is, in fact, another list of positive traits that are much too rarely discussed. The advantages of ADHD may include being:

- enterprising
- driven – someone who gets things done
- energetic – having virtually boundless energy
- creative and good at thinking outside the box
- fearless and willing to pursue new ideas
- curious
- flexible
- able to hyperfocus
- persistent – someone who won't give up but keeps trying
- intuitive
- good at thinking laterally – having an ability to see things from new angles
- good at shrugging off setbacks – not one to dwell on mistakes

This book is about the positive traits – that is, the advantages. But why is there a need for such a book? Hasn't enough been written about ADHD already? I think that the more we emphasise the problems and forget the positive aspects, the greater the risk is that we will create new problems for those with ADHD. By 'new problems' I mean low self-esteem and a feeling that many of the doors in life are closed to you; that there are things you can't do.

If, on the other hand, we emphasise the advantages, I think we can achieve the opposite result: improved self-esteem and a sense that many doors are open. Because having ADHD means having a different – and unique – toolbox that you must learn to use.

At the same time, I want to stress that the list of positive traits is a rough generalisation and not everyone with ADHD possesses all of them – in the same way that not everyone struggles with everything on the list of difficulties. Yet there is no doubt that these positive traits are more common among those with ADHD than in the population at large.

ADHD is a wide grey area

'Surely, I have ADHD, don't I?' The 23-year-old sitting in front of me at my clinic looks almost imploringly at me. It's evident that he expected to leave here with an ADHD diagnosis after the assessment he has just undergone. He struggles to hide his disappointment.

'It's true that you have some traits that are characteristic of ADHD,' I say, without detecting the slightest hint of his disappointment diminishing. 'In fact, we all have traits of ADHD and fall somewhere along an ADHD spectrum. You probably rank above average on the spectrum, but your symptoms and difficulties aren't severe enough to warrant a diagnosis.'

He looks even more puzzled. 'What do you mean *"traits* of ADHD"? Either I have ADHD or I don't, right?'

The young man points to one of the greatest medical misconceptions of our time: that either you have ADHD or you don't at all. In his defence, it's not surprising that he thinks this way. Not a day goes by without newspapers and the media reporting on ADHD, often as a diagnosis as clearly delineated as HIV or a heart attack.

While ADHD is indeed a medical condition, this doesn't mean that a clear line can be drawn between 'healthy' and 'sick'. Without implying any similarities between HIV and ADHD, other than that both are medical diagnoses, you can't have 'a touch' of HIV. Either you have it, or you don't – but you can most definitely have 'a touch' of ADHD.

ADHD can be compared to physical height. After all, it's not like everyone is *either* short *or* tall; most people fall somewhere in between. The same applies to concentration issues, impulsivity and other ADHD symptoms, which – like height – are distributed variably among the population. Some people have almost no trouble concentrating, while others struggle a lot, but most fall somewhere in the middle.

So, where do you draw the line between ADHD and 'normal' concentration issues? That's the million-dollar question. Where do you draw the line for tallness in men? At 1.89m? Or 1.84m? There is no simple answer to that question. Just as there is no simple answer to where we should draw the line for ADHD. There are no blood tests or X-rays that can show if you have ADHD. Instead, we use a checklist on which certain criteria must be met. In addition to having issues with concentration, impulse control and hyperactivity, as mentioned above, these issues should cause problems in your life and daily activities. And it's not enough to struggle, say, only in school – that could be due to a poor study environment. Rather, the problems should be noticeable both at home and at school or in the workplace. What's more, these issues must have persisted since childhood, because ADHD isn't something you develop as you get older; it's something you'll have had all your life.

To be diagnosed with ADHD, you must thus have experienced *severe* problems as a result of concentration issues and impulsivity – but what does that mean? Do you not have ADHD if you have trouble concentrating but still managed to obtain an academic degree? Again, there is no unequivocal answer to that question.

In practice, what constitutes 'normal' concentration issues on the one hand, and ADHD on the other, is a wide grey area. It's in the borderland between 'normal' concentration issues and ADHD that we have witnessed a shift in recent years, with more and more people being added to the ADHD side. Slowly but surely, we have come to believe that all restless and lively children – and adults, too, for that matter – have ADHD. As a consequence, we have started to think that these problems are best solved with diagnoses and medication. To extend the height analogy, it's as if, year after year, we have lowered the bar for what counts as being tall.

Different names for the same thing

Issues with concentration and hyperactivity are, of course, nothing new. The term ADHD – attention deficit hyperactivity disorder – was coined in the 1980s, but this wasn't the first time a diagnosis was given to these types of difficulties. In the late 1700s, the Scottish physician Alexander Crichton referred to the symptoms as 'mental restlessness' and described vividly how some students were so bored with grammar that not even the threat of a beating could persuade them to pay attention in class: 'Every public teacher must have observed that there are many to whom the dryness and difficulties of the Latin and Greek grammars are so disgusting that neither the terrors of the rod, nor the indulgence of any kind in treaty can cause them to give their attention to them.'

A century after Crichton, the wildly misleading label 'abnormal deficit of motor control' was often applied to what we now call

ADHD. In the 1940s, it was described as 'minimal brain damage' (MBD) – an even more fallacious term that is unfortunately still in occasional use today. In the 1970s and 1980s, it was known as 'deficits in attention, motor control and perception' (DAMP), before we finally settled on ADHD.

These different diagnoses are not just historical curiosities. Within psychiatry, the percentage of the population believed to meet the criteria for these conditions has varied significantly, even though they fundamentally describe the same thing. For instance, it was once estimated that 1 per cent of all children had MBD. In the case of DAMP, it was thought to be around 2–5 per cent, while in the US in 2023 around 11 per cent of all children and adolescents (aged 4–17) were diagnosed with ADHD. With such big fluctuations, it's not surprising that the condition has had to change its name from time to time. After all, it wouldn't seem very serious to initially claim that 1 per cent of children have MBD but then all of a sudden change it to 10 per cent.

These constant name changes reflect the grey area I have described, where the boundary of what constitutes the condition has gradually shifted. The different names also indicate how perceptions of what we now call ADHD have varied – ranging from the result of a shoddy upbringing to full-on brain damage. Hopefully, we will eventually come to recognise all these historical diagnoses as more or less incorrect and understand that ADHD is, in fact, a normal variation in human behaviour. Quite simply, it is a set of personality traits that has been crucial in humanity's evolution and that in modern society can present both challenges and advantages.

IS ADHD MORE COMMON IN BOYS?

More boys than girls get diagnosed with ADHD, but does that mean more boys actually *have* it? We can't know for certain. Girls with ADHD have trouble concentrating and struggle to direct their attention, but they tend not to act out or be as hyperactive as boys. This means their symptoms may not be as noticeable, leading to an underdiagnosis of girls with ADHD – who, as a consequence, don't receive the help they need.

The complexity of human nature

As if it weren't enough that we all have traits of ADHD, we also have traits of other psychiatric conditions. We have bipolar traits and consequently fall somewhere along that spectrum, too. People with few or weak bipolar traits have a stable mood, while those with strong traits experience significant mood swings. (Being bipolar doesn't mean that your mood changes from one day to the next but rather from month to month, swinging from depression to mania.) What's more, we all have some traits of autism and fall somewhere on that spectrum as well. This doesn't mean that we are all bipolar and autistic, of course, but rather that such conditions are often challenging to delineate.

Does that sound complicated? It is. Human nature *is* complicated! But really, it's no stranger than the fact that we aren't only tall or short but can also be thin or overweight at the same time.

The point is that it's important not to overgeneralise. People with ADHD aren't all alike, just as everyone else isn't either. We are far more complex than can be encapsulated in a single condition.

CAN YOU OUTGROW ADHD?

Previously, it was thought that only children could have ADHD and they eventually grew out of it. Today, we know that's not the case and that ADHD persists into adulthood in more than half of those who had it as children, albeit with a slightly different expression in adults. For instance, hyperactivity seems to diminish, while concentration issues persist. And what about the other half? Do they grow out of it? The truth is we don't know. What's clear, however, is that the regions in the brain that are crucial for concentration and impulse control mature late and aren't fully developed until around the age of 27. This contributes to the way traits of ADHD may appear to fade in some individuals.

I also think there is another reason why ADHD is more common in children than adults, and it's that adults have more control over their lives. An adult who is impatient and restless can avoid a job where meticulous precision and routines are crucial. An adult can choose to do something where other qualities are valued. Children have a much more limited scope to choose how to shape their own lives. For a child who doesn't do well in the classroom, it can be tough – the flexibility to control their daily life is often lacking.

Can you develop ADHD as an adult? This question is hotly debated, but it seems that people are born with ADHD and it doesn't develop later in life. However, it may very well be that ADHD symptoms become more pronounced as a person gets older and the school or workplace environment becomes more demanding, making it seem as if the symptoms are only just emerging. If a person suddenly experiences severe concentration issues in adulthood, it's important to identify the underlying cause, as conditions like depression and anxiety may also lead to trouble concentrating.

One diagnosis – several biological causes

All people have some traits of ADHD. To complicate things further, research shows that ADHD can have a variety of different causes in the brain. Outwardly, they take on a similar expression, with concentration issues, impulsivity and hyperactivity, and so we group them together and slap a single label on the whole lot. To extend the comparison with HIV: if you have HIV, you have been infected with a virus, and everyone who has HIV carries the virus. That's not the case with ADHD. Since ADHD is a medical condition, you might think it would be well defined and have the same underlying cause in everyone, but it's not that simple.

But wait, isn't this a book about the *advantages* of ADHD? What do grey areas – not to mention a hardship like HIV – have to do with it? What I want you to understand before we continue is that it's difficult to draw a clear line around what ADHD is. Since we all have some traits of it, what I describe in this book won't apply only to people with ADHD but to a great many others as well.

To better understand this, let's start by taking a look inside the organ where all your thoughts, feelings and behaviours originate. The organ that *is* you: your brain.

ADHD OR ADD – WHAT'S THE DIFFERENCE?

If a person experiences significant concentration issues and is impulsive without being hyperactive, this is sometimes known as attention deficit disorder (ADD). People with ADD often come across as absent-minded and dreamy but they are not hyperactive (that is what the 'H' in ADHD stands for). Typically, they don't struggle to sit still, which means ADD isn't as obvious as ADHD – after all, hyperactivity is rather easy to spot.

Those with ADD don't stand out as clearly in environments like school, which often leads to the condition being entirely overlooked or only diagnosed later in life. Just like with ADHD, there isn't a clear boundary for what constitutes ADD as opposed to 'normal' issues with concentration and impulsivity.

CHAPTER 2

A MORE BORING WORLD

We are just another species – albeit a rather peculiar one.
And we will never understand ourselves unless we
understand how our natures evolved.

MATT RIDLEY, BIOLOGIST AND AUTHOR

WHAT DRIVES YOU? Is it love, money, validation or security? Perhaps it's seeking new experiences or pushing yourself to the extreme – hurling yourself down steep mountain slopes on skis, sky-diving or running long-distance races?

In a crude clinical sense, the answer is simple. What drives you is a tiny cluster of neurons deep within your brain, about the size of a pea. In medical jargon, this 'pea' is known as the nucleus accumbens, but in everyday speech it's often referred to as the brain's reward centre. Everything you enjoy – whether it's savouring delicious food, spending time with friends, listening to music, getting a 'like' on Facebook, having sex or going for a run – starts here.

When mentioned in the media, the reward system is often

described as a neuroscientific curiosity, a part of the brain that lights up like a Christmas tree when we have sex, eat delicious food or get promoted at work. In reality, this system plays a much more significant role than merely providing a sense of pleasure. The reward system – the nucleus accumbens – doesn't suddenly switch on when you receive praise from your boss and then switch off. It's constantly simmering.

When you are listening to a lecture, there is a certain level of activity in your reward centre. The same goes for when you are reading or listening to these words. If the activity level in your reward system drops, you will find the text boring and unconsciously start thinking about other things that might activate it – perhaps your phone, which has an incredible capacity to trigger it. If the lecturer drones on and you feel a strong urge to pick up your phone, it's your nucleus accumbens that is contributing to that urge.

The nucleus accumbens is continuously letting you know whether what you are doing is worth your time. If it doesn't think so, you'll feel a hankering to do something else. In other words, the nucleus accumbens tells you whether the lecturer – or this text – is interesting enough to keep you reading or listening.

Certain things activate the reward system in most people, including good food, socialising with others and sex. But there are also things that affect the reward system differently from person to person. My reward system fires up when I listen to music, but it's stone dead if I'm forced to watch sport on TV. The fact that the reward system is triggered by different things in different people isn't all that surprising; after all, we all have different tastes.

Some individuals seem to have a reward system that functions a little differently from birth. It's simply slower, which means that what's sufficiently stimulating for most people won't activate their reward system. Instead, they need bigger experiences than sitting and listening to someone talk, watching TV or reading a newspaper article. It's as though their engine requires more fuel to start – and by 'more fuel' I mean more intense experiences.

To these individuals, the world seems dull and uninspiring. What's a little boring for most of us is unbearable for them. If tackling German grammar was a challenge for me in high school, for them it's simply insufferable. Their reward system – whose job it is to tell them if something is interesting enough to keep doing – is saying: 'What the teacher is talking about up there isn't interesting enough, keep searching,' or, 'This article I'm reading isn't interesting either, keep searching.' And searching is precisely what they end up doing. They are constantly on the lookout for an experience, big or small, that can activate their reward system. And so, of course, they can't stay focused. 'Is there anything interesting over there? No. How about here? No. What about over there? No, not there either. Keep searching!'

A person who is constantly jumping between various stimuli comes across as unfocused and scattered, and may also become impulsive and hyperactive. Starting to sound familiar? That's right: it's ADHD.

A reward system that's different, not inferior

It seems pretty obvious that being unfocused may have negative consequences in today's society. How is it, then, that some people have a reward system that is less active? Could there be a reason for this difference and that our ability to concentrate thus varies from person to person? Probably, but in order to understand why, we'll need to rewind the clock.

Imagine two of your ancestors out on the savanna, searching for something to eat. One of them has an insufficiently activated reward system. The slightest rustling in the bushes, the tiniest gust of wind – everything grabs his attention. 'What's that? Nothing. How about that? Nothing either. But that over there?' and so on. This ancestor who constantly scans his surroundings is intensely aware of everything happening around him. His brain doesn't filter out a single sensory input, making him conscious of them all – no matter how small or insignificant they may seem.

Now, let's turn our attention to the other ancestor. While he is focused on hunting for food, his brain filters out many irrelevant sounds and stimuli. For example, he doesn't hear the rustling leaves, which are probably just the wind but could also be a rabbit. Of course, he would notice if an antelope or a lion suddenly appeared a short distance away, but his brain filters out a little rustling in the bushes. Who do you think stands a better chance of catching food and surviving? My bet would definitely be on the one who is hypersensitive! Nine times out of ten, the rustling leaves are nothing more than the wind – but the tenth time it might just be a rabbit that could become a meal.

The hypersensitive individual probably had the best chance of success on the savanna. Now, let's continue our thought experiment by transporting both ancestors into today's world and placing them in a classroom or an office. How would they fare here? Now it's suddenly not as clear that the hypersensitive one would have the advantage. The heightened sensitivity to stimuli that allowed him to react to the rustling in the bushes might suddenly become a disadvantage. He can't hear what the teacher is saying because a classmate coughs, someone moves their chair or a car passes by in the street.

The second ancestor, on the other hand – who is better at filtering out irrelevant information and therefore failed to spot the rabbit or the lion – will find it much easier to concentrate on what the teacher is saying. Now the roles are reversed. The trait that was an advantage on the savanna suddenly becomes a hindrance in the classroom or office.

Many ADHD patients I have met describe precisely this: they can't concentrate because they are constantly being sidetracked by everything else. The tiniest thing can distract them and it's impossible to resist the temptation to look: a fan humming, a ticking clock on the wall or a person coughing four rows down in the lecture hall. Not to mention their ever-present mobile phone. It's like the volume for sensory stimuli is always turned up high. And as if that weren't enough, hundreds of thoughts are racing through their mind. All of this disrupts and tugs at their concentration.

The example invoking our ancestors shows that you can't automatically say that having an increased sensitivity to stimuli is a disadvantage. There and then, it might very well have been an advantage. After all, the person who spotted the rabbit everyone else missed got food, thus increasing his chances of surviving and passing on his genes.

But, suddenly, we have completely overhauled our way of life. We have left the savanna, stopped hunting for food and replaced that world with one where we can order dinner online at the push of a button. We have transitioned from the savanna to Facebook in 10,000 years and, while that might sound like an eternity, from an evolutionary perspective it's a blink of an eye. Our brains have hardly changed at all. In other words, we are still adapted to life on the savanna, but several of the personality traits that helped us back then may now be a burden.

Could it be so simple that what we now call ADHD was, in fact, an adaptation to our historical way of life? An adaptation that used to bring advantages but turned into a disadvantage when we swiftly changed our lifestyle? I believe that is precisely the case – though, of course, my beliefs or opinions don't prove anything. So is there any concrete proof to suggest that ADHD could have been an advantage? In fact, there is. Let's take a closer look at your brain's reward system – your innermost driving force – to understand how this 'pea' that propels you through life actually works.

A strong craving for dopamine

When we talk about activity increasing in the reward system, what we mean is that dopamine levels are rising. Dopamine is passed from one brain cell to another, thereby transmitting a signal between them. More dopamine in the reward system makes you feel good, but for dopamine to have an effect, it must bind to a receptor. Receptors serve as a kind of docking station for dopamine. Dopamine docks in the receptor and initiates a reaction that culminates in a sense of wellbeing.

The dopamine receptors we all have in our brains can look different from person to person and be more or less effective at binding dopamine. If the receptors function well, you'll feel a clear sense of wellbeing from the dopamine. If they are less effective at binding dopamine, you may not experience the same sense of wellbeing. How your dopamine receptors function can, therefore, affect how you feel. In fact, it may influence your whole personality.

There is a type of dopamine receptor known as dopamine receptor D4 (DRD4). Both you and I have DRD4s in our brains, but yours may not necessarily be identical to mine. That there can be small differences between them is not really any stranger than the fact that we differ in hair colour and height.

Some people have, from birth, a variant of DRD4 known as DRD4-7R. What's special about this receptor is that it's not as active when dopamine binds to it. It's as if the key – that is, dopamine – fits a little less well into the lock – that is, DRD4-7R. For this reason, someone born with the DRD4-7R variant has a reward system that works a bit differently.

Let's say you and I have different DRD4s. I have DRD4-7R, the variant that isn't as active when dopamine binds to it, while your variant responds more strongly when dopamine binds to it. Imagine that we are both watching the same TV programme and our brains are releasing roughly the same amount of dopamine. For me, the result is that my reward system is activated to a lesser extent, and as a consequence I'll probably find the programme a bit less exciting. Since my dopamine receptors don't react as strongly, I need more dopamine to achieve the same effect. In other words, what makes you feel good doesn't have the same effect on me.

Since dopamine is crucial for the reward, I'll be walking around with a reward system that is insufficiently activated. I will try to compensate for this by giving myself more dopamine – that is, seeking out things that provide a bigger dose. I will have a strong craving for quick dopamine hits. To summarise, someone born with the DRD4-7R variant has a less active reward system and, as a result, will likely perceive the world as being a bit more boring.

ADHD isn't caused by poor upbringing or the wrong diet

Even though it's often difficult to draw a clear line between ADHD and 'normal' issues with concentration and impulsivity, one thing is clear: ADHD primarily results from biological factors and from the brain functioning in a slightly different way. ADHD is not a result of upbringing or a lack thereof – a misconception that unfortunately lives on – nor is it caused by diet, allergies or a fast-paced society. Of course, factors like a disruptive study environment can lead to concentration difficulties resembling ADHD, and may be misinterpreted as such, but fundamentally they are not.

How can I state this with such confidence? The biggest reason is that ADHD is hereditary. Whether or not you have ADHD largely depends on whether your parents have it. Here you might object and say that, if your parents have ADHD, perhaps you are simply mimicking their behaviour, and therefore it doesn't necessarily follow that ADHD is biologically determined. That's a valid response, but after studying both identical and fraternal twins, we know it's not that simple. Identical twins have virtually identical genes. If one of them has ADHD, the likelihood that the other also has it is around 70 per cent. Fraternal twins, on the other hand, have genes that are as different as regular siblings' – so if one of them has ADHD, the likelihood that the other also has it is only 30 per cent. The significant difference in these figures, even though twin pairs usually grow up together, strongly indicates that ADHD is something you inherit.

Another factor supporting the heritability of ADHD is the slight differences in the brain observed in individuals with ADHD – in fact, certain parts appear to be somewhat smaller. This doesn't mean that individuals with ADHD are less intelligent, as there is no correlation whatsoever between brain size and intelligence. Besides, the differences in size are very minor. What it strongly suggests, though, is that ADHD is largely a result of our biology.

COULD THERE BE SOMETHING ELSE BEHIND IT?

ADHD is primarily influenced by our genes, but concentration issues and impulsivity can, of course, also be caused by factors other than what's happening in a child's (or adult's) brain. A chaotic classroom situation or excessive mobile phone use could also lead to symptoms that resemble ADHD and are misinterpreted as such. Likewise, if you have experience something truly awful and develop post-traumatic stress disorder, it too can lead to difficulties concentrating. When conducting an assessment, it's therefore crucial to thoroughly examine whether there might be some other underlying cause for concentration issues, impulsivity and hyperactivity.

But if ADHD is largely hereditary, does that mean the environment is unimportant? No, because even though heredity and genetics are probably the most significant causes of ADHD, our environment can interact with our genes. How our DNA – that is, our genome – is expressed is influenced by the environment we live in. This interplay between nature and nurture is incredibly complex. Even though we aren't close to fully understanding it yet, it's clear that many psychiatric conditions are not primarily caused by *either* our environment *or* genetics, but by a combination of both. One can imagine inheriting a vulnerability to a condition like ADHD, but whether it actually develops depends on the environment in which you grow up.

ADHD is hereditary

So, ADHD is largely hereditary. In fact, there are hardly any other medical or psychiatric conditions where heredity – i.e. our genes – plays such a big role. Researchers worldwide are working hard to understand which genes are involved in causing ADHD, and there are several that seem particularly important. One gene that comes up in study after study is called DRD4-7R. Both the gene and the dopamine receptors I mentioned previously share the same name. This is because someone born with this gene will have DRD4-7R receptors in their brain – and a less active reward system. Thus, they are at an increased risk of having ADHD.

One thing is clear: the genetics of ADHD is complex. DRD4-7R alone doesn't determine if you have ADHD – instead, many genes come into play. Four others that are important are DAT1, DRD5, DBH and 5HTR1B. As you can see, genes often have complicated names consisting of abbreviations. But what do three of them have in common? Three out of four begin with a 'D'. And what do you think the 'D' stands for? You guessed it: dopamine!

In one way or another, these three genes – much like DRD4-7R – also affect dopamine in the brain. The more we learn about the genetics behind ADHD, the clearer it becomes that the brain's reward system and dopamine play a crucial role in ADHD. For example, it has been found that individuals with ADHD may not only have different dopamine receptors; they can also have *fewer*. This likely has a similar effect as when the receptors function poorly. If there are fewer dopamine receptors, dopamine won't be able to exert its effects as there is nothing for it to 'dock' into. It even seems that the fewer dopamine receptors a person has, the greater their difficulties concentrating.

It's not just the brain's reward centre that is affected by the DRD4-7R receptors' reduced response when dopamine binds to them. There are also DRD4s in the frontal lobes – the part of the brain located behind the forehead, the seat of our impulse control and ability to stay focused. The altered functioning of DRD4-7R receptors also impacts the effects of dopamine in the frontal lobes, which is believed to further contribute to ADHD symptoms.

Quick dopamine hits

'What seemed interesting enough for everyone else in school, I found boring – so I made noise, disrupted class and pulled people's hair. Looking back, I realise I was searching for a reaction; otherwise I would have died of boredom. It's always been like that. I need to feel engaged and alive, all the time.'

I don't know how many variations on this theme I have heard from ADHD patients over the years. They have all explained that they have found the world far too dull. They have been constantly understimulated and, more or less consciously and with varying consequences, tried to compensate for it. As soon as nothing is 'happening', they lose focus.

So, many people with ADHD have an insufficiently activated reward system and will constantly try to kick-start it – after all, the system is the engine for everything we do! More or less subconsciously, they impatiently scan their surroundings and seek out things that will raise their dopamine levels.

And what raises dopamine levels in our brain? Many things do, and it also varies from person to person, but the following tend to boost dopamine levels in most people:

- food
- strong sensory stimuli and intense experiences
- sex
- the Internet and mobile phones
- drugs like cocaine and amphetamines

Food addiction, binge eating, sex addiction, Internet and video game addiction, extreme sports and drug abuse have all been found to be more common in people with ADHD. An insufficiently activated reward system makes you 'short-sighted' – not visually, but rather in the way you think. The brain is simply wired for quick dopamine hits, and it wants them now.

A less interesting world

One of the main reasons why drug abuse, Internet addiction, sex addiction and binge eating are more common in people with ADHD is probably that they are compensating for an insufficiently activated reward system through their behaviour. But this doesn't mean that everyone with ADHD – or those who rank highly on the spectrum – becomes an addict or sits glued to their computer. Such compensation can take entirely different forms.

Workaholics thrive in the fast lane, when the world around them is spinning rapidly. To make life exciting and stimulating enough, they jump from one task to the next. They don't feel at their best when they have finished a task but while they are doing it, or even just before starting. In others, this drive can take the form of creative expression, such as a desire to make something – perhaps on an artistic level. This trait normally doesn't fade with time, as you get older or your circumstances change. I have seen restless and hardworking entrepreneurs achieve great financial success and decide to finally 'kick back'. Now they plan to read books and travel! Six months later, they feel awful – as empty inside as they are bored. The driving force they have had all their life doesn't just vanish because their bank account is full.

I believe one and the same mechanism can underlie behaviours like alcohol, sex and Internet addiction, workaholism and a strong creative drive. It's the inability to find the world exciting enough as it is. This constant restlessness stems from not wanting to stay in the 'now' that is felt to be too boring. The American psychiatrist John Ratey has described these individuals as having 'an itch they can never scratch'.

Naturally, the consequences of having an insufficiently activated reward system may differ. Those who can channel their impatience into work, sport or an artistic project have the potential to become incredibly successful. If, instead, they try to manage it with alcohol, drugs or gambling, things can end badly. For those with too little dopamine, there are both good and bad ways to try to get more. In this book, I will focus on the good.

Digital drugs

The next time you step onto a bus, a train or the metro, conduct a little experiment: count how many people are *not* staring down at their phone. I amuse myself with this from time to time, and I can usually count a maximum of two or three people per train car. Almost everyone is lost in their phone these days.

The American neuroscientist and author David Linden believes the Internet is tailor-made to cause addiction. He compares it to training a dog. Suppose you want to teach your pup to sit, and you have a chunk of meat at your disposal. You could say 'sit' and give the dog the whole chunk of meat if it heeds your command. This will trigger the dog's brain to release large amounts of dopamine, making the dog feel great. As a result, it will obey you when you say 'sit' tomorrow – but how long will this last if the dog doesn't get a new chunk of meat every time? Two weeks later, there is a good chance the dog will have forgotten all about it and will choose to ignore you. Another option is to divide the meat into hundreds of tiny pieces. Every time the dog obeys and sits, it's rewarded with a small piece of meat. The dog is unlikely to be overjoyed, but it still gets a small dopamine hit each time.

The second strategy works best. It's more effective to repeat the connection between the behaviour (the dog sitting) and a smaller reward (a tiny piece of meat) than to give the whole chunk of meat at once. When you divide the meat into lots of tiny pieces, you will, thanks to repetition, get a perfectly trained dog that obeys you immediately.

The Internet works exactly the same way, says Linden. Each 'like' on social media provides a small dopamine hit in the brain's reward system – not very significant, but enough for us to register it as positive. A Facebook 'like', for instance, doesn't provide a big reward (the whole chunk of meat) but rather a smaller one (a tiny piece). Yet when it's repeated hundreds of times, a clear association is created in your brain between the behaviour – looking at your phone – and the arrival of a small dopamine hit. This is precisely what makes you feel a strong urge to reach for your phone as soon as a TV show isn't maximally interesting or the person you are talking to becomes too long-winded.

For a person with ADHD, the digital world is particularly seductive. If you have an insufficiently activated reward system, the small dopamine hit you get from your phone can be incredibly alluring. Putting TikTok or Snapchat in the hands of someone with a sluggish reward system is like holding a bottle of water in front of a person who has just run 10km on a scorching summer day. It's simply irresistible.

Since our mobile phones are tailor-made to activate our reward system, teachers face increasingly tough competition for children's attention. The contrast between the classroom and the digital world is becoming enormous. The digital world is thus not the *cause* of ADHD – but for a person with strong ADHD traits, the temptations and quick rewards of, say, their mobile phone will make school feel especially boring.

Dopamine makes the world interesting

The role of dopamine is not just to make you feel good but also to guide you towards different behaviours by telling you whether something is worth doing. What's fascinating is that dopamine actually has a wider role than simply informing you that something is positive and worth your time and focus. It also applies to negative things. If you were to find yourself in a dark alley with an angry Doberman, you would have no trouble concentrating. Whether your phone chimed with a text message or you heard a car starting nearby, you wouldn't take your eyes off the dog. In this situation, dopamine ensures nothing can distract you. Even when it comes to negatively charged experiences like the threat of an angry canine, dopamine makes sure that we maintain our focus.

In other words, dopamine is not just a 'pleasure substance'; it also ensures that we have the motivation to direct our focus, whether it's towards something positive or something negative. A little philosophically, you might say that dopamine puts us in connection with the world around us and makes us interested in it. In essence, dopamine makes the world more interesting.

An intriguing question is what would happen if we didn't have dopamine. Most likely, we wouldn't survive. When scientists modified the genes of mice so that their brains could no longer produce dopamine, they became completely apathetic and preferred to starve to death than open their mouths. Even when food was placed right in front of their noses, they had zero motivation to get up and eat. If they were given a dopamine injection, however, they suddenly started eating normally again. In other words, dopamine tells animals – just like you and me – whether something is worth taking an interest in. When dopamine is entirely absent, nothing is interesting. Not even eating if you are starving.

Low dopamine levels render things and experiences uninteresting – you lack the motivation to follow along with what the teacher is writing on the board or to listen to what your colleague has to say.

Therefore, ADHD leads not only to poor concentration but also to poor motivation. The distinguished psychiatrist Nora Volkow has even suggested that ADHD ought to be renamed 'attention and motivation deficit disorder' (AMDD) to emphasise that it's not just the ability to concentrate that is impaired but also your motivation.

Drugs hijack the dopamine system

Proponents of drug liberalisation who think that society's strict views on narcotics equate to scaremongering should take a closer look at the reward system. For there is nothing that activates the system as effectively as drugs. In fact, all addictive drugs directly target the reward system and raise dopamine levels in the nucleus accumbens in an incredibly treacherous way.

If a plate of food is placed in front of you when you are hungry, your dopamine levels rise, motivating you to eat. Let's say that you eat until you are full, and then more food is presented. Now your dopamine levels are no longer affected in the same way. The fact that you aren't hungry any more means the food no longer triggers the same activity in your reward system.

With a drug like cocaine, for instance, it doesn't work this way. If you place cocaine in front of a drug user, their dopamine levels rise and they feel a strong craving for it. Let's say they take the cocaine – and then more is offered. Now, the new cocaine will trigger the same amount of dopamine to be released in the reward centre as the first time. It creates the same craving, even though you have already taken the drug.

You can take the drug five or ten times in a short period, and each time it will produce an equally significant spike in dopamine levels. There is no end, no sense of being full. The drug 'hijacks' a system that evolution has meticulously honed over millions of years. The intense dopamine surge the drug creates in the reward system is virtually unattainable by natural means. Nor can natural stimuli generate such a powerful, repeated dopamine kick without causing a feeling of being satisfied or 'full'. It's not at all surprising that so many people struggle with narcotics, since nothing kick-starts our reward system in quite the same way.

Who do you think might be particularly vulnerable to this? A reasonable guess would be those individuals who already have a lower activity level in their reward system from the outset. For them, the activity the drug creates can be absolutely enormous, and the craving for the drug extremely intense. It has been found that alcohol and drug abuse are more common in people with ADHD – which, of course, is not the same as saying that all people with ADHD are addicts. However, what it does mean is that people with ADHD should be especially careful with drugs.

Self-medicating

One should be extremely careful when using the terms 'self-medication' or 'self-medicating', which are often used to excuse oneself from personal responsibility in cases of substance abuse. However, after meeting a large number of patients abusing amphetamines and cocaine, I believe that's precisely what many of them are doing. They are more or less unconsciously compensating for a reward system that has functioned differently from birth. Many of them have exhibited clear signs of ADHD since childhood, and have, not least, been impulsive since long before they started using.

There are good and bad ways to get your dopamine fix. Drugs are undoubtedly the worst.

Food and drug addiction don't sound like they belong in a book about the advantages of ADHD, so why am I bringing this up? It's because I want to explain the crucial role the reward system plays in our behaviour, and how it functions differently in many people with ADHD – which can lead to problems. But every coin has two sides, and it's time we flip from the downside to the upside: what might be the advantages of having a different reward system and the traits we call ADHD? To understand that we'll have to start by turning back the clock.

CHAPTER 3

NATURAL WANDERERS

*In just 50,000 years we covered everything. There is a kind of
madness to it. Sailing out into the ocean, you have no idea what's
on the other side. And now we go to Mars. We never stop. Why?*

SVANTE PÄÄBO, EVOLUTIONARY GENETICIST,
NOBEL LAUREATE

OPEN A WORLD MAP and look at all the cities strewn across it.
With a few exceptions, there are people everywhere on earth – but it
hasn't always been this way. Just 60,000 years ago, the majority of
the world's population was found in East Africa. The species to which
you and I belong, *Homo sapiens*, was one of several human species,
and our homeland was the regions we now call Ethiopia, Kenya and
Tanzania.

We undoubtedly hold ourselves in high regard today, but on the
savanna humans weren't so special. There was little to suggest the
impact we would come to have on our planet. We were one of
many species, neither more nor less significant than any other, until

suddenly something happened. In less than 50,000 years – a short period in an evolutionary context – our ancestors spread from Africa to all corners of the globe, colonising every continent. First, they went northeast to the Arabian Peninsula and the Middle East, then onwards into Asia, north into Europe, east across Asia and Russia, eventually reaching North America. Then they journeyed south through North and South America, even making it to Australia and New Zealand. Fifteen thousand years ago, there were people on all of earth's continents.

We don't know for sure what prompted our ancestors to suddenly leave their homelands and venture into the unknown. Why didn't they stay in Africa? And once they had found a new continent to settle on, why did they continue to explore further, generation after generation, instead of staying where they were? Why did they cross the Bering Strait from eastern Siberia to North America? Why did they set out to sea without knowing what awaited them, eventually reaching as far as New Zealand?

It is of course difficult to find definitive answers to these questions, but it likely wasn't only external factors such as conflicts, natural disasters, changes in climate and food shortages that drove them – even though such factors must often have contributed. It's likely it also had to do with an internal drive to explore.

So, what was this drive that led them to continue exploring until there were no uncharted territories left on our planet? This behaviour is completely unique; no other species does anything like it. If there is enough food and space, other animals typically stay where they are and don't move on just for the sake of it. Other human species – such as the Neanderthals – did not behave in such a way. They tended to stay in one place for much longer. Why venture into the unknown when there is enough food where you are? You know what you have but not what you'll get, so why risk it?

Clearly, this is not how our ancestors reasoned; they instead left the familiar for the unknown, impatiently seeking new and unfamiliar territories. They weren't satisfied until they had explored the entire planet, and their curiosity undoubtedly paid off. Seventy thousand years ago, there were between 100,000 and 300,000 people on earth. Today, we number more than 8 billion, which means there are at least 26,000 times as many of us now.

If our ancestors had chosen to stay in one place without moving about, and thereby failed to make space for a growing population, the likelihood of you and me existing would be minuscule. We can thus consider ourselves lucky that our ancestors possessed this drive to explore. Not all humans did so, however – some never left Africa in the first place. Among those who reached the Middle East, some chose to settle there, while others continued on to Asia and beyond.

During these migrations, groups continuously split up, with some people settling while others continued to wander. This pattern has persisted for tens of thousands of years. Thanks to archaeological and historical research, we have learned a great deal about how people migrated across the world. We know that some groups have moved more than others, and it's not a matter of how physically active they were or how far they journeyed within a single generation – but rather how far they travelled over hundreds of generations. Specifically, the distances they covered in the last 30,000 years.

People in South America are among those who migrated the farthest in that time, while in Asia and Scandinavia people have been more likely to stay put. So, can we find any differences between those who moved great distances for hundreds of generations and those who tended to stay where they were? It seems we can. The difference lies in our genes – in a specific gene that affects the brain's reward system. It's the same gene you read about in the previous chapter and that is associated with having a less active reward system. It is the same gene that's linked to ADHD: DRD4-7R.

The long migration

A few years ago, researchers examined more than 2,000 people from around 30 different regions across the world. The study included members of the Cheyenne tribe in North America, Brazil's indigenous Karitiana people, the Mbuti in Congo and the Maya in Mexico. Others hailed from places not quite so exotic, including Finns, Swedes, Italians and Spaniards.

Among these roughly 2,000 individuals, there were vast differences in lifestyle. They ranged from city dwellers in Europe and rural hunters in South America to Australian Aboriginals. A broader spectrum of human ways of life is hard to imagine. Yet these people from all corners of the earth differed not only in their current lifestyles but also in how their ancestors had lived historically – especially in terms of how far they had migrated. Some had ancestors who moved vast distances over hundreds of generations before finally settling where they live today. Others had ancestors who were more likely to remain in one place for thousands of years.

When their genes were examined, it turned out that the variant of the DRD4 gene that you read about in the previous chapter, DRD4-7R (the one that makes the reward system more 'sluggish'), was more common among populations with a history of migrating across vast areas. The further these populations had moved in the last 30,000 years, the more common DRD4-7R was among them. The same pattern was observed across all continents.

This suggests that if many people in a group have the gene, that population has been inclined to migrate. Since the gene seems to propel people to seek out previously unknown places, it has been dubbed the 'explorer gene'. But where do we find those who have the gene today, when there are essentially no places left to discover on earth? What are they doing? In this context, it's fascinating to note that DRD4-7R is especially common among people with the condition this book is about: ADHD.

Could it be that those who have ADHD today possess personality traits that have historically contributed to humanity spreading across the globe? I believe that's precisely the case – but before we proceed, a caveat. One must always be cautious when drawing conclusions from this type of research. Individual genes don't determine our personality traits. They contribute to them, sure, but they don't dictate them. The environment plays a significant role, too.

What's more, population movements are extremely complex. There can be many reasons why people choose to migrate – conflicts, food shortages or climate change, to name a few. For someone whose livelihood depends on farming a crop that can no longer grow due to a cooling climate, it's natural to consider packing up and moving on. The same is true if a competing group of people settles a couple of kilometres away or if a pride of lions happens to roam nearby.

Besides, it often takes much more than just a 'thirst for adventure' to explore new lands. Setting sail into the unknown requires more than a little bit of 'wanderlust'. You also need a sturdy boat, and building such a vessel requires advanced skills that no single gene can provide, let alone the same gene that makes you inclined to explore new places in the first place.

In other words, the drive to explore cannot be reduced to a single gene, so DRD4-7R alone cannot have been the sole cause for our exploration of all corners of the earth. But there is much evidence to suggest that the gene – and the personality traits it contributes to – has played a significant role as a driving force. The same pattern emerges everywhere you look: the further a population has travelled in the last 30,000 years, the more common the DRD4-7R gene is among them. If we observed a correlation between how far a population has historically wandered and how common the gene is in only *one* place on earth, it could be explained by chance – but the same pattern is observed among people all over the globe.

How common is the gene in different parts of the world?

If a people has travelled long distances in the last 30,000 years, DRD4-7R – which I'll also loosely refer to as the 'ADHD gene', even though ADHD isn't caused by a single gene – is more common among that population today compared to areas where people have not migrated quite as far.

Location	Percentage of the population who carry DRD4-7R
Europe	15
North America	20
South America	50–70
Japan and China	0–5

THE ADHD ADVANTAGE

In South America, a high percentage of the population carries the ADHD gene – somewhere between 50 and 70 per cent. But does that mean ADHD is more common there than on other continents? The prevalence of ADHD actually seems to differ between different countries, and South America is the continent where ADHD is most common, while significantly fewer people have it in, say, Asia.

The DRD4-7R gene is particularly common in South America, and a particularly high number of people seem to have ADHD there. Is there a connection? The answer is that there might be – but we must be careful when drawing conclusions from this type of finding. Comparing the prevalence of ADHD in different countries is extremely difficult, because in addition to any genetic differences, there can be cultural reasons, such as stigma attached to seeking help for psychiatric problems and the availability of mental health clinics, as to why the number of people diagnosed with ADHD varies. What's more, other genes than DRD4 are also important for ADHD. Should the fact that only a small portion of the Chinese population carries DRD4-7R be interpreted as meaning that ADHD doesn't exist there? Certainly not. Chinese children have ADHD too, but very few of them carry DRD4-7R, which isn't surprising since the gene is very rare in Asia. However, they do carry a similar gene, called DRD4-2R, which biologically seems to function similarly to DRD4-7R – meaning it doesn't respond strongly to dopamine.

A link to our past

It's reasonable to suspect that the personality traits and characteristics that contributed to humans leaving Africa and spreading across the world are the same traits we now call ADHD. But is there anything more concrete to suggest these traits have been an advantage historically? Something we can measure today? Indeed, there is. A vital puzzle piece is revealed if we turn our gaze to the desert of northern Kenya and the Ariaal people.

The tribe's roughly 1,000 members live the same way today as they did thousands of years ago, herding livestock. Normally, they don't stay in one place for more than a few weeks; they continually roam in search of food. Their existence is a constant struggle; they must track new prey, capture it and then move on. Sometimes the hunt goes well, but often it fails, leaving them hungry. Many members of the tribe are malnourished, with an average body mass index (BMI) of 17–18, which by Western standards counts as being underweight (the range for normal weight is 20–25). The Ariaal people's way of life is so far removed from what you and I are accustomed to that it's nearly impossible to imagine. Yet from a historical perspective, it's not the Ariaal whose lifestyle is unusual – it's yours and mine. Humans have lived like the Ariaal people for all but the entirety of our existence.

Imagine lining up all your ancestors in a direct line going back a million years. (If you are a woman, it would be your mother, grandmother, great-grandmother and so on; if you are a man, it would be your father, grandfather, great-grandfather and so on.) This would be about 50,000 people – the population of a medium-sized Swedish town. Of these, 49,500 lived as hunter-gatherers, like the Ariaal people, while barely 500 were farmers. Only you and about ten others have lived in an industrialised world. For the vast majority of your ancestors, your lifestyle would seem incredibly peculiar – which is entirely true from a historical perspective.

The Ariaal people are one of the last groups on earth who still live in a similar way to your ancestors. Although not all hunter-gatherers lived the same way all over the world, the Ariaal nevertheless serve as a unique link that helps us to understand our own history. But even for them time has not stood still – in recent decades the tribe has split. One group has broken away and settled in one place to live as farmers, while the others continue to roam as hunter-gatherers.

It has been observed that among both the hunters and the breakaway farmers who now practise agriculture, there are tribe members who carry the DRD4-7R variant (the ADHD gene), while others carry a variant of DRD4 that cannot be linked to ADHD. In other words, the ADHD gene has been found among some of the farmers and some of the hunters, which in itself is not unexpected. What *is* unexpected is that hunters carrying the ADHD gene are more well nourished than hunters who do not. Individuals with the ADHD gene appear to be better at finding food than those without the gene. And to be clear, 'well nourished' in this context does not mean overweight – since members of the Ariaal tribe are typically malnourished, it means that they are one step further away from starvation. The fact that some of them have a higher BMI likely indicates that they are more successful hunters.

Among those who are farmers, however, those with the ADHD gene are more *malnourished* than those without it, thus farmers with the ADHD gene seem to be less successful finding food. Taken together, all this suggests the ADHD gene was an advantage for those of our ancestors who were hunters, but a disadvantage for those who were farmers.

ADHD means having trouble concentrating, but also being impulsive and acting immediately without thinking. Could this, too, be explained by our origins on the savanna? There are reasons to suspect so. The American author and psychotherapist Thom Hartmann has described it as 'behavior preceding cognition' – acting first and thinking later. On the savanna, constantly scanning your surroundings and reacting lightning fast to anything you might eat or that might eat you may be a matter of life and death. The same impulsivity doesn't work quite as well in the classroom or the office.

Farmers vs hunters

Let's pause for a moment and contemplate the personality traits that make for a good hunter and how these traits differ from those that are beneficial to a farmer.

A hunter on the savanna must be extremely vigilant or there is a risk they will miss potential prey. At the slightest sign of something interesting, they must act immediately, almost on impulse. If they aren't quick enough, the rabbit might hop away or the lion might launch an attack.

For a farmer, however, it's less important to be constantly vigilant and able to make split-second decisions. Farming involves long-term decision-making, after careful analysis of the situation. What crops should we grow this year? Should we have more cows or focus on goats instead? These decisions have significant consequences in the long term, but no immediate impact. Executing what you have decided requires planning and consistency. If you are going to grow a specific crop, it's best to stick with it and not keep changing your mind – otherwise there is a risk that nothing will be accomplished at all. It's easy to see that qualities that make for a good hunter don't necessarily make for a good farmer.

A hunter needs to be good at:

- adapting to a changing environment – being able to quickly switch strategy if circumstances change
- making swift decisions and reacting immediately and instinctively
- reading their surroundings to be able to react quickly to critical things, like a sudden threat
- being hyperfocused when something is genuinely important
- seeing the results of their decisions in terms of what happens within seconds or minutes

A farmer needs to be good at:

- living in one place
- making long-term decisions and not reacting instinctively and hastily
- planning for the long term and sticking with an idea
- ignoring distractions
- managing routines and not getting bored when every day is the same
- making decisions based on what will happen months or years from now

As you can see, a good hunter and a good farmer have almost opposite qualities. You don't need to generalise too broadly to conclude that it's the qualities of a farmer, rather than a hunter, that are rated most highly in our modern society. Yet for most of our history we have lived as hunters – 49,500 of your 50,000 ancestors were, in fact, hunters.

The traits that characterise a person with ADHD are being easily distracted, impulsive, impatient and driven, having a lot of energy and always being 'on the go'. They also have a constant need for stimulation, a dislike of routines and the ability to hyperfocus for brief periods of time. These traits align almost perfectly with the qualities that make for a good hunter, suggesting that the traits we now call ADHD have probably been important – maybe even crucial – to our survival during the vast majority of human evolution. Yet suddenly, in only a few hundred years, we have made enormous changes to our lifestyle, creating a society in which these traits don't fit quite as well.

The transition from hunting and gathering to agriculture meant that life changed significantly – and not necessarily for the better. It probably became duller and more monotonous. Being out hunting every day is varied: it involves roaming around, seeing new vistas and tracking different prey. Being a farmer means staying in one place, and each day being pretty much the same as the next.

One can't help but wonder why people all over the world made the leap from hunting to farming if life became more predictable and less varied. The answer is probably that farming is more efficient, and through agriculture more mouths can be fed. The same surface area of land can yield more food – and the differences are substantial. Some have calculated that it's possible to feed ten times as many people with agriculture as with hunting.

The danger of an evolutionary perspective

Trying to understand human traits and conditions from an evolutionary perspective is fascinating. Why do we become depressed? Why do we suffer from allergies? Why do we cry when we are sad? Why do so many people have ADHD? Researchers have attempted to answer all these questions by examining our origins, and in each case they have arrived at explanations that seem not only possible but also plausible.

If we have experienced a long period of severe stress, our brain interprets a world full of stress as one that is dangerous to live in. We may then suffer with depression, which becomes a survival strategy when our brain tries to isolate ourselves from the outside world and avoid others by creating feelings of sadness and withdrawal.

We develop allergies because modern humans live in an overly 'clean' world while also possessing a potent immune system. When it isn't exposed to enough dirt, bacteria and viruses, it goes berserk over grass pollen and cat hair. We cry to signal that we care about others, or that we need help. The reason why so many people have ADHD is that historically it has been an advantage to possess the personality traits associated with the condition.

But even though an evolutionary perspective is fascinating and offers plausible explanations, we must be cautious since it's often hard to prove whether such explanations are actually true. So, is it just a wild guess that ADHD could have served as an advantage for humans historically? I don't think so. The reason I don't think it is just a baseless guess is the genetic findings you have read about herein – namely that a gene linked to ADHD is more common among those who have migrated great distances, and the same gene remains an advantage in hunter-gatherer societies today.

Children of survivors

There is another, more fundamental reason supporting the idea that ADHD has been advantageous: evolution eliminates traits that cause problems. In fact, evolution is ruthless. If the traits we call ADHD had only been a hindrance, the individuals who possessed them would not have survived. They wouldn't have had children and passed on their genes. ADHD would have gradually disappeared, or at least been culled until it became rare – and that's not what we see today.

You and I are so accustomed to having a roof over our heads and food on our table that we have stopped reflecting on it, but for the vast majority of people who have walked this earth, life has been a constant struggle for survival, and those who couldn't adapt perished. Half of all humans died before reaching adulthood for 99.9 per cent of our history. Only the ones who survived disease, famine, natural disasters and wars had children and passed on their genes.

At times, humanity has been dangerously close to extinction. One such bottleneck is believed to have occurred some 74,000 years ago, when the climate suddenly cooled after a massive volcanic eruption on the island of Sumatra in Indonesia spread its ashes across large parts of the globe. Genetic evidence suggests that, at the darkest hour, there were only a few thousand people left in the entire world! Your ancestors and mine were among the few who endured, ensuring the survival of our species.

In fact, your ancestors and mine have survived time and time again throughout history. You and I are the latest generation of an unbroken line of ancestors who did not succumb prematurely to disasters, starvation, accidents, disease or predators. It's therefore safe to say that personality traits that are common today must have been important for survival during human history, otherwise those who had them would have died out. The fact that the traits we call ADHD are common today is therefore *in itself* a strong indication that they have historically been an advantage.

Errors – evolution's crucial tool

The human migration out of Africa is believed to have started approximately 60,000 years ago, but why then? Why not 100,000 years earlier or later? It might have been due to the colder climate, but there is reason to believe that the answer at least partially lies in our genes.

Evolution has a crucial tool at its disposal when developing different species, and that tool is error. In fact, if nature didn't make errors from time to time, there would be no evolution – and you and I wouldn't exist. So, what is this error on nature's part that paved the way for our existence?

When the cells in our bodies divide, each cell's DNA must be copied in its entirety, which involves more than 3 billion genetic letters. An enormous amount of genetic information is copied every time a new liver cell, blood cell or brain cell is formed in your body. This copying process is incredibly precise, but not perfect. Occasionally, an error slips in. Most of the time the error is inconsequential, but in rare cases it can cause harm – in a worst-case scenario, a genetic miscopying can lead to cancer.

On even rarer occasions, the erroneous copying can – by pure chance – lead to an improvement, such as when a miscopying in the gene for red blood cells makes the cells in question *better* at transporting oxygen to the organs. We are unlikely to notice an improvement in a single red blood cell as we have trillions of them; the effect of only one blood cell is minuscule. However, if this incorrect DNA copying occurs in a sex cell – that is, in a sperm or an egg – the miscopying will be inherited by the next generation, whose blood cells will *all* become better at binding oxygen. This results in a child who has better stamina and thus a survival advantage.

In this way, errors in gene copying have slowly shaped all species over millions of years. Genetic miscopies that confer an advantage and increased chances of survival are passed on to the next generation. Those who are affected by these errors increase their chances of survival, while the errors that lead to disadvantages are eliminated since those affected by the latter instances of miscopying don't survive in the same numbers and are less likely to pass on their genes.

More common than by pure chance

Another term for errors in gene copying is *mutation*, and today it's believed that DRD4-7R (the ADHD gene) – just like all other mutations – came about purely by chance. It was simply an error in the copying of the genetic material in one of our ancestors. The mutation resulted in the affected individual having a slightly less sensitive reward system, which in turn made them more impatient and restless. The consequence may have been that they constantly surveyed their surroundings and reacted quickly at the slightest sign of something happening, which was an advantage when hunting. This meant the person had a greater chance of surviving. They passed on their genes to their children, who in turn passed the mutation on to theirs. Over time it gradually spread to more and more people and became more common among the population.

Some mutations are thought to have occurred millions of years ago, while others took place relatively recently in evolutionary terms. Today, scientists can estimate when a mutation occurred in our evolution using advanced genetic technology, and it's estimated that the mutation that created DRD4-7R belongs to the latter category – it's quite recent in human evolution. It appears that DRD4-7R began to spread around 40,000–50,000 years ago (the gene may have existed prior to this, but it seems it started spreading widely around 50,000 years ago). This is approximately the same time that humans began to leave Africa. Is it just a coincidence that this happened simultaneously? Perhaps, but the timing has led scientists to speculate that there could be a connection. Possibly, the mutation and the personality traits it contributed to mark the actual starting shot for humanity's spread across the world. In fact, it could mean that we wouldn't have left Africa at all if it hadn't been for DRD4-7R.

If this sounds speculative, let's imagine a seemingly insignificant mutation that arose in recent history and began to spread among humans around 10,000 years ago. Such a mutation would usually be uncommon in today's population since it hasn't had much time to spread – after all, it only emerged 10,000 years ago. A mutation that occurred, say, 1 million years ago (around 400 generations) will be found in more individuals as it has had a long time to spread.

If you know when in history a mutation occurred, you can calculate how common a specific gene should be among today's population. If it's more common than it should be, you can suspect that it probably brings advantages. If it's less common than it should be, it likely confers disadvantages. It has been found that about 20 per cent of all people on earth carry the DRD4-7R gene. This means it's significantly more common than it should be considering that it emerged just 50,000 years ago. The fact that DRD4-7R is carried by one-fifth of all people, despite being relatively recent from an evolutionary perspective, is yet another strong indicator that the gene *has* provided, and *continues* to provide, advantages for those who have it.

Why doesn't everyone have the ADHD gene?

Globally, there are significant variations in how common the ADHD gene is. But as you can see, there is no place on earth where everyone has it – not even in hunter-gatherer societies like the Ariaal people in Kenya. Despite the gene appearing to make it easier to catch food, only some members have it – not all. But why doesn't everyone have the gene if it makes you better at catching prey? The answer is probably that humans are social animals. We live in groups with others and are good at different things – these are the conditions around which evolution has shaped us. Everyone benefits from someone in the group being extremely adventurous and taking risks, but we also benefit from someone else being cautious and planning ahead. If everyone were adventurous and took risks, life would be utter chaos. At the same time, we wouldn't make any progress if everyone were overly cautious and risk averse. It seems there is a balance to be struck, not only for our ancestors, but in today's society, too. Some people have the gene and the traits it contributes to, but not everyone. We are *meant* to be different.

Mass migrations and tribes on the savanna may seem a far cry from our daily lives in the here and now. So what consequences do the traits we call ADHD and the DRD4-7R gene have today? We'll take a closer look at that in the next chapter.

CHAPTER 4

AN ENGINE FOR CURIOSITY

Many attributes of our restless, anxious modernity, perhaps, are products of a restless, anxious gene.

SIDDHARTA MUKHERJEE, *THE GENE*

IN A PSYCHOLOGICAL EXPERIMENT, a group of young men were given $250 each, which they could wager on a coin toss. A loss meant they would lose everything they had wagered, while a win would result in a 150 per cent return. The men were free to choose how much they wanted to bet, and unsurprisingly there were significant differences between them. Those who didn't like taking risks played it safe and refrained from betting, and consequently went home with their $250. Those who were true risk-takers bet the full $250 and went home either empty-handed or with a substantial profit ($625).

Take a moment to consider what you would have done. Would you have gone all in or cashed out immediately? Or would you have done something in between, and if so, what? Regardless of how much you would have chosen to bet, what do you think your choice would have depended on? One thing is certain, it's not just a matter of the environment you grew up in; your genes also play a part. When the men's genes were examined, it turned out that – you guessed it – DRD4-7R (the ADHD gene) was linked to how willing they were to take risks. Those who carried the gene were more inclined to wager a larger sum and were thus more willing to risk their money. In fact, the gene accounts for 20 per cent of the hereditary part of our inclination to take risks. In psychological research, it is rare – extremely rare, even – for a single gene to contribute so significantly to one trait.

Let's move on. Do you like skiing? For me, it's one of my favourite things to do, and every time I go skiing I'm struck by how differently people behave on the slopes. Some take risks and love speed skiing or flinging themselves down steep slopes, off-piste. Others are more cautious and prefer gentle slopes where they can avoid going at high speeds. Of course, this depends on how skilled they are as skiers, but could it also have something to do with their genes? It actually appears so, as it has been found that a certain gene is more common among those who enjoy extreme off-piste skiing: DRD4-7R. Other variants of DRD4 (that is, non-ADHD variants) are much more common among those who are perfectly content to skid around on the green slopes.

Genes, politics and swans

How prone you are to risk-taking in wagers and on the ski slopes is just the beginning – DRD4 has also been linked to our political views. When the genes of more than 2,000 individuals were examined, along with their reported voting habits, it turned out that DRD4-7R was more common among those who vote liberally. Scientists have speculated that individuals with this variant of the gene may be more sensation seeking, curious and adventurous – more open to new experiences and more social. Their personality traits lead them to interact with many different people and expose themselves to different world views and lifestyles. Meeting a diverse range of people who live in different ways tends to inspire an open-minded attitude, making the curious person more likely to vote liberally.

This might sound like mere speculation, but it has been demonstrated on several occasions that the DRD4 gene is correlated with our political leanings. Another study found that those with DRD4 variants *not* linked to ADHD were more conservative than those with the ADHD gene. But don't interpret this that nature has endowed us with either liberal or conservative genes. Instead, our genes influence our personality traits and people with different personalities may, in turn, be more or less inclined towards different political views.

As if it weren't enough that DRD4 has been linked to political views in humans, research has shown that the gene also affects animal behaviour. DRD4-7R is more common among swans (yes, they have it too!) living in urban environments than in rural areas. The researchers' aim was to study whether the gene influenced how brave the swans were.

So how do you determine if a swan is brave? Simply by observing how close you can get to it before it takes flight. Brave swans allow people to approach more closely, while cautious swans take off when you are still at a considerable distance. It turned out there was a significant difference between urban and rural swans. The swans in rural areas took flight at a distance of 96 metres, whereas those in the urban park didn't take off until the researchers were only 13 metres away.

This can partly be explained by the fact that swans in urban waterways are more used to people, but there is also thought to have been a form of behavioural selection between rural and urban swans. Swans in cities that are afraid of people simply fly away to find a quieter place to live. Consequently, particularly 'brave' swans – which are more likely to carry the DRD4-7R gene – have congregated in urban areas.

Interestingly, a similar pattern has been observed in other animals, including Siberian huskies and *Chlorocebus* monkeys, where the DRD4 gene appears to affect impulsivity. Just like humans, dogs and monkeys can also have different personality traits – some are impulsive and active, while others are more cautious. And their level of caution has been linked to which variant of the DRD4 gene the animal carries. The gene that makes humans more thrill-seeking appears also to influence the bravery of swans and dogs.

Thirst for adventure

Research on political views, skiers, swans and dogs might seem disparate. Is it really possible for a gene to fully explain how you behave on the ski slopes or how you vote? No, of course not. Genetics is immensely complex, and personality traits cannot be fully explained by individual genes or genetics altogether, whether in humans, swans or dogs. Naturally, the environment – that is, your surroundings – also plays a significant role.

Nevertheless, it's interesting to note that the same gene keeps cropping up in areas that fundamentally revolve around our propensity for risk-taking and seeking out new experiences, both in humans and other species. When examining the findings individually, we shouldn't jump to major conclusions, but taken together, you can't help but feel that they reveal something fundamental. DRD4 plays a crucial role not only in risk-taking but also in our desire to experience new things – what's often referred to as 'novelty seeking'.

People who have the DRD4-7R variant of the gene appear to be more inclined to try new things and avoid the predictability of routine. Twenty thousand years ago, the unknown literally lay beyond the next valley. Today, we know what's there; a quick glance at Google Maps will tell us. Now, a thirst for adventure expresses itself in new ways, such as wanting to ski in rugged places or making risky investments.

It might seem strange that a trait as complex and crucial for us humans as the desire to seek new experiences could be influenced by dopamine receptors on the surface of our brain cells. These structures are so small – measured in millionths of a millimetre – that they can't even be seen using a microscope. Indeed, it's astonishing that all our memories, dreams and emotions arise inside a kilogram-heavy organ that looks like tightly packed sausages – that is, the brain. It's almost impossible to grasp that microscopic differences in the brain can affect our lives and personalities.

When I learn more about this research, I sometimes get the dizzying feeling that I'm peering into the machinery of the soul. I not only feel that I understand the mechanisms that shape me a bit better – it also suddenly makes more sense why the personality traits we call ADHD are so common in today's society. At the risk of repeating myself one time too many, it's important to remember that ADHD isn't caused by *one* gene but *many*. DRD4-7R is one of the most well-studied genes linked to ADHD, and I use it here to illustrate that what we call ADHD has likely been an advantage historically.

Does all of this mean DRD4-7R only brings advantages? No. Just like many other genes, DRD4-7R can confer both advantages and disadvantages. The gene is, for instance, linked to an increased risk of alcohol and gambling addiction. One should be wary of painting a condition like ADHD in too rosy colours, and the same goes for the DRD4-7R gene. It contributes to personality traits that can indeed be positive but that may also be expressed in destructive ways.

What's best for the group

Let's conduct a thought experiment: imagine a group of calm and cautious children entering a room where sweets have been hidden in various places. Some are in the drawers of a dresser, others are under the rug and a couple have been concealed behind a picture on the wall. How long do you think it will take them to discover all the sweets? Probably quite a while. Now, let's say the children are restless and hyperactive. How quickly can they find the sweets? I would venture to guess that they'll find them considerably faster than the calm children.

Consider what's happened historically when we have arrived at new places. Having a few restless and impatient individuals in the group meant they could quickly search the area and maximise the resources available in that location. In other words, it was important for a few people to quickly scan the place for anything edible. Since information can easily be transferred from one person to another – and it can, thanks to our advanced capacity for language – it's enough for a few individuals to possess these traits. What they find can then be used by everyone.

If you have ADHD, it might be little consolation to hear that your personality traits would likely have been a hit on the savanna, or that they can be linked to risk-taking in modern times. So let's leave history behind and focus on the advantages ADHD can offer in today's society. We'll start with what might be humanity's most highly prized trait: our creativity.

CHAPTER 5

CREATIVE DAYDREAMERS

There is something nonlinear in how the ADHD brain
functions – a kind of lateral thinking that opens
things up to big ideas.

DALE ARCHER, PSYCHIATRIST AND AUTHOR

IMAGINE AN ARTIST WHO completely dominates the hip-hop scene, whose songs consistently top all the charts and who has single-handedly transformed the entire genre – someone all other hip-hop stars are inspired by and try to emulate. Now imagine that the same artist is equally influential in hard rock, electronic dance and pop music. Imagine that, in passing, they have also written some of the most timeless soul and R&B classics. They are a musician who excels in practically every musical genre – and they have achieved all of this before the age of 35. Does this person sound too good to be true? The fact is such a person did exist, and his name was Wolfgang Amadeus Mozart.

Mozart lived to be only 35 years old, yet he managed to

compose more than 600 works of music. What's most impressive, however, isn't the quantity he created but his versatility. He composed symphonies, operas, choral music and piano concertos, mastering every genre to perfection.

If you read about the Austrian composer's turbulent life you will notice that a few characteristics come up time and again: he was energetic, impatient, easily distracted, impulsive, demanding and lacked any and all respect for authority. This list essentially contains all the traits we now associate with ADHD. Can we say for certain, then, that Mozart had ADHD? No, we can't. Many people amuse themselves with diagnosing historical figures, and while it can be tantalising to do so, it's extremely precarious to attempt to diagnose a person you have never met. Therefore, there is no definitive answer as to whether the most legendary composer of all time had ADHD.

The personality traits said to have characterised Mozart have also been mentioned in reference to a long list of other creative geniuses, including writers like George Bernard Shaw and Edgar Allan Poe, the artist Salvador Dalí and the inventor Thomas Edison – the latter having both the light bulb and the phonograph on his CV.

As with Mozart, it is impossible to say with any certainty whether Shaw, Poe, Dalí or Edison had ADHD. But is it a coincidence that creative individuals of this calibre are often described in ways that are reminiscent of ADHD? An American researcher decided to delve deep into this area and conducted a thorough review of the field of creativity research since the 1960s. The conclusion was that there are 16 personality traits that are common in creative individuals. Among them are being energetic, risk-taking, curious, independent and emotional. Sound familiar?

The 16 personality traits that are common in creative individuals as well as individuals with ADHD make it tempting to suspect that people with ADHD are more creative. But for proof of a link between ADHD and creativity, the 16 traits are not enough. We would instead have to test whether individuals with ADHD are, in fact, more creative. And to conduct such tests, we must first define what creativity really is. What does it mean for someone to be more creative than others, and how can you measure it?

Good at brainstorming

One thing is clear, and it's that creativity is complex – perhaps the most complex of all our cognitive abilities. There is no measure or test that encompasses all conceivable aspects of creativity. Instead, there are a range of tests that measure different dimensions of our creative ability. The most classic creativity test involves being given a word like 'paper clip' and then being asked to come up with as many uses for that object as possible in the shortest time. For this test, it's not enough just to come up with lots of ideas; they must also be reasonable and, ideally, no one should have thought of them before. The test is conducted under a time constraint and measures what is known as 'divergent thinking' – essentially brainstorming, the ability to generate lots of new ideas.

To investigate whether there is a connection between ADHD and creativity, a group of students were gathered – some had ADHD and some did not – and asked to participate in various creativity tests. It quickly became apparent that, on average, those with ADHD were better at divergent thinking. Not only did they come up with more suggestions for any given word, their suggestions were also more varied and more original. These students therefore excelled at brainstorming. Yet, interestingly, in creativity tests that emphasised logic they were *not* better – often they were worse. One interpretation is that people with ADHD are not as cognitively inhibited as those without ADHD and they don't restrain their stream of thoughts. This is an advantage when brainstorming, but it can work against you in tasks that require more logical thinking.

One may wonder if the connection between ADHD and brainstorming also applies to children. This was tested by showing a group of children – some of them with ADHD – a number of toys. They were then told that a toy company needed their help to come up with entirely new toys, and they only had five minutes to think of ideas.

Naturally, one cannot expect children to come up with revolutionary ideas for new toys in just a few minutes, and that's not the point. What the researchers were primarily looking at was whether the children merely copied one of the toys they had just seen or whether they could come up with something that wasn't a copy. Showing examples before asking a person to come up with new ideas has been found to have a negative impact on creativity. Most of us fixate on what we have just seen and copy it, but truly creative individuals can ignore the examples and not let themselves be limited by them.

What's measured when children are asked to come up with new toys is essentially their ability to overcome the obstacle of prior knowledge to think new and creative thoughts. So, what did the researchers find? The children with ADHD didn't copy the toys they had just seen but came up with more original suggestions – they were simply more creative. A similar result occurred when university students brainstormed after they were presented with a number of examples:

students with ADHD found it easier to overcome the examples and thus performed better than their peers without ADHD.

These experiments show that both children and adults with ADHD appear to be more creative when it comes to what we call brainstorming. But what is it in the brain that underlies this?

The daydreaming brain

Lift your gaze from the page for a moment and lean back. Relax and try not to focus on anything; let your thoughts wander freely. What comes into your mind? Perhaps you are thinking aimlessly about your day so far. Maybe you are contemplating what to have for dinner or what the weather will be like tomorrow.

What do you think happens in the brain when you daydream like this? Does it relax and become less active, like a mobile phone in standby mode? One might certainly think so, but that's not the case. In fact, some areas of the brain become *more* active when we are passive and let our thoughts wander. These areas, located in various parts of the brain, are interconnected in a network commonly referred to as the brain's 'default mode network' (DMN).

Simply put, the DMN is your 'daydreaming brain' – the parts of the brain that are active when you aren't doing anything in particular. It's believed that DMN generates a flow of spontaneous thoughts, a stream of consciousness. The DMN works actively when you engage in an inner monologue with yourself, like deciding whether you are in the mood for lasagne or sushi for lunch, or contemplating whether a darker wallpaper would be better in the living room. When you eventually transition from daydreaming to actually doing something – let's say your boss interrupts your lunch or interior design ruminations and asks you to write an email – the activity in the DMN decreases. Instead, the brain's executive parts, known as the 'executive network', come to life. These parts, which include functions like planning and impulse control, activate in your brain when you write the email.

Normally, the brain's executive areas are not active at the same time as the daydreaming ones; it's either one or the other. The DMN – the daydreaming part of the brain – shuts off when the executive part turns on, and vice versa. It's important that it shuts off and makes room for the executive part. If it doesn't, and they are both active at the same time, you will be distracted and unfocused when you try to write your email – and that's precisely what seems to happen to individuals with ADHD. When they decide to write the email, the DMN doesn't turn off but remains active at the same time as the executive part of the brain. The daydreaming part doesn't leave the stage and make room for the executive part but remains there, distracting them. Simply put, the 'off switch' for the brain's 'daydreaming programme' seems to be slower in people with ADHD.

The DMN might seem like something as mundane as daydreaming dressed up in fancy neuroscientific jargon. You might also get the impression that the DMN doesn't serve a purpose – why has evolution equipped us with a part of the brain dedicated to daydreaming that can disrupt our concentration? Couldn't we just as well do without it? Well, it's not that simple. The DMN is neither a disturbance nor a curiosity; it provides a spontaneous stream of ideas in the brain that appears to be central to our creativity.

When researchers examined the brains of improvisational jazz pianists, they found increased activity in their DMN, but when the musicians played from sheet music, their DMN didn't activate in the same way. This phenomenon has also been observed when comparing brain activity in rappers who freestyle and those who rap written lyrics. The more improvisation that's involved, the more active the daydreaming brain will be.

The daydreaming brain thus appears to be crucial for creativity; it's activated when we engage in something creative. It's believed that individuals with ADHD struggle to turn off their daydreaming brain, which may be a key explanation for why they are often more creative in certain areas. Though there may be other reasons, too.

Easily distracted creative talents

One way to understand whether creativity can be linked to ADHD is to use various creativity tests. Another is to investigate what distinguishes those who are particularly creative – and that's precisely what researchers did in a study of around 100 students at Harvard. Some of them had received awards for composing music, painting or writing poetry or fiction. The researchers referred to them as 'eminent creative achievers'.

If you were researching what makes someone creative, what personality traits would you choose to investigate when comparing individuals who have received awards for their creative achievements with those who have not? Personally, I might consider examining whether their IQ differs, to see if those who are more creative are also smarter. The Harvard researchers chose to look at something entirely different: the individuals' ability to ignore distractions. Are especially creative individuals better – or worse – at disregarding disruptive noises, for example?

If one were to guess the outcome in advance, it would be no big leap to assume that creative people are good at ignoring distracting sounds – that they can become so swept up in their creative work that they are nearly impossible to distract. But as it turns out, the opposite is true. The creative individuals weren't better at ignoring distractions, but worse. Strangely enough, those who had difficulty ignoring a whirring fan were more creative. And the differences were substantial; those who struggled to ignore disruptive sounds and distractions were seven times more likely to be classified as eminent creative achievers.

But how can it be an advantage for your creativity to be easily distracted and disturbed by fans and other sounds? A plausible explanation is that some people hear the fan, recognise it as uninteresting and unconsciously filter it out. After a while, they no longer think about it. While their brain continuously registers the fan, the information doesn't reach their consciousness and the noise is filtered out. Others perceive the sound as if it were something new and interesting all the time, since their brains are not as good at filtering out irrelevant information. In scientific jargon, this phenomenon is called 'leaky attention'.

Interestingly, leaky attention seems to go hand in hand with an increased stream of thoughts and an enhanced ability to think outside the box – that is, creativity. These people not only notice the fan, they take in all other information as well, and the more information and thoughts reach their consciousness, the more creative they become. A person who filters out the fan also filters out thoughts that may potentially be important for their creativity. Someone who is disturbed by the fan may indeed have more unimportant thoughts, but they can also have more thoughts that turn out to be significant in the end. Leaky attention helps us integrate ideas and thoughts

THE ADHD ADVANTAGE

that are outside our current area of focus. Sometimes these are entirely unimportant – like the fan – and sometimes they are crucial. If you are easily distracted, which many people with ADHD are, there is a possibility that you are also more creative.

When you think about it, it's not surprising that leaky attention and the intense stream of thoughts that it brings can be important for creativity. In a creative process, you often don't know in advance what will be important. What might initially appear irrelevant when you are writing a book, trying to come up with a new recipe for a cake or starting a business may turn out to be the crucial puzzle piece that makes everything fall into place in the end. If you have a brain that absorbs a lot of information and sees all stimuli as potentially interesting, it increases your chances of eventually seeing things in a new light and coming up with ideas others wouldn't. What makes someone creative is thus not that they are easily distracted but that they are more mentally open and flexible. They absorb more information and more stimuli, and the more they absorb, the greater the possibility of connecting information and stimuli in unexpected and novel ways.

So, what does leaky attention have to do with ADHD? Well, many people with ADHD have wider attention. They pick up on more than others and are more aware of what's going on around them. They seem to lack the filter that screens out not only distractions and noise but also, perhaps, unusual ideas. They have leaky attention.

The thalamus – our mental gatekeeper

Let's take a closer look at how leaky attention works. Your brain is constantly processing vast amounts of information from your senses: auditory, visual and tactile stimuli: how hot or cold it is; if a car is honking outside; how your clothes feel against your skin. In addition to sensory stimuli, it also receives information about how your body's organs are functioning. Right now, all this information is reaching your brain, but the fact that you are unaware of most of it is crucial to preventing sensory overload. How your socks feel or the noise coming from a fan is not typically something you need to consciously think about.

To prevent ourselves from being overloaded by sensory stimuli, there is a kind of 'mental filter' deep within the brain, known as the thalamus. The thalamus receives information from various parts of the brain, including the centres for vision, hearing and touch, and it serves as a gatekeeper that selectively determines what information should be allowed into your consciousness.

For instance, imagine you are in a meeting room at work with your boss, discussing your new list of responsibilities. You would probably pay close attention to your boss and not attach much importance to the fan humming in the background or the discomfort of your chair. Focusing your attention solely on the fan and the chair while disregarding your boss could jeopardise a pay rise or promotion! Your thalamus is essential to filtering out distracting sensory stimuli like these.

There is a molecule that plays an important role in helping your thalamus function properly, and having read this far you can probably already guess what it is: dopamine! Dopamine is not only crucial for motivation and reward in the brain, it also plays a vital role in the thalamus, affecting the amount of information that passes through it. As you already know, many individuals with ADHD seem to have a different dopamine system, which is believed to result in the thalamus working less effectively, causing them to be overwhelmed by sensory stimuli. Many of my patients with ADHD describe a constant stream of thoughts and impressions, as if the brain's volume control for sensory stimuli were turned up to the max.

However, the permeability of the thalamus is influenced not only by dopamine but also by other factors, such as the gene known as 'patched domain containing 1' (PTCHD1). The function of this gene has long been a mystery. We knew *that* it affects a person's risk of having ADHD, but not *why* it has that effect – until 2016, when a group of scientists discovered that PTCHD1 influences the thalamus. The version of the gene that is common among people with ADHD appears to make the mental filter in the thalamus work less effectively, thus turning up the brain's volume control for sensory stimuli.

When mice were exposed to a flashing light in connection with being fed, they quickly learned to associate the light with mealtimes. If they heard a sound signal that was not followed by food a couple of times, they rapidly learned to ignore it. They reacted to the flashing light but paid no attention to the sound. Yet after modifying their PTCHD1 gene, the mice struggled to discern which information was important and reacted to both the sound and the flashing light. Why? It turned out their thalamus worked less effectively. Because of the alteration to PTCHD1, the mice became overwhelmed by sensory stimuli and struggled to focus on what was essential – in this case, the flashing light.

Both dopamine and the PTCHD1 gene thus appear to affect how much information the thalamus lets through and how good the brain is at filtering out irrelevant 'noise' from our sensory stimuli. But why am I complicating things by bringing this up? Because mice who struggle to choose which stimuli to focus on often, but not always, benefit from ADHD medication that increases their dopamine levels. The medication thus allows most, but not all, mice to suddenly concentrate on the flashing light and learn to ignore the sound signal. Researchers wondered why not all mice become better at filtering out irrelevant information. It turned out that this positive effect of medication could *not* be observed in the mice with a mutation in the PTCHD1 gene. That's probably because it was the gene, and not a lack of dopamine, that was the cause of their sensory overload. More dopamine – the result of the ADHD medication – didn't have the desired effect because it wasn't dopamine deficiency that was the problem.

We know that ADHD medications are effective for about 60–70 per cent of all people with ADHD. But why not for everyone? The answer may be that not everyone with ADHD has a dopamine deficiency and, for them, more dopamine won't help. The mice with a mutation in PTCHD1 didn't respond to the medication because the cause wasn't a lack of dopamine. The fact that the brain's mental gatekeeper – i.e. the thalamus – can be influenced by a gene *and* by dopamine levels is thus an example of how several different mechanisms in the brain can produce the symptoms we call ADHD. Outwardly, the symptoms may appear similar – difficulty concentrating, hyperactivity and impulsivity – but the causes in the brain may differ.

So how can you determine the cause in a patient with ADHD? You can't. When diagnosing and treating ADHD, clinicians must rely on what they can observe – the symptoms. Perhaps it will one day be possible to investigate these mechanisms so that everyone can receive tailored treatment that addresses the root cause in their brain.

CAN MEDICATION MAKE ME LESS CREATIVE?

Even though it's impossible to say for sure whether Edison, Mozart or Dalí had ADHD, it can safely be stated that we would all be worse off if individuals of their calibre didn't have an outlet for their creativity. ADHD medications can help you to become better at ignoring distractions. What's more, when ADHD is treated with medication, the activity decreases in the brain's daydreaming network, the DMN. Given that both the DMN and the inability to disregard distractions are linked to creativity, one might wonder if we risk medicating away the creativity of children and adults. Might we have missed out on the creativity of Mozart, Edison and Dalí if they had been diagnosed with ADHD and been medicated? It's conceivable, and some scientists have warned thus, but we don't yet know with 100 per cent certainty.

I have had several patients who chose to stop taking their medication because they felt it made them less creative. A musician told me his guitar playing became mechanical and dull when he was medicated. While he didn't make mistakes, he felt that his playing was less inspired and that he often fell into the same repetitive patterns. He struggled to 'think outside the box' and come up with more unconventional ways of playing, so he discontinued his medication. He considered the loss of concentration that resulted from this to be a price worth paying. However, I have also seen patients who have been *better* able to channel their creativity when taking medication.

It has helped them to overcome the obstacles that ADHD can present, making them better at both creating structure and working patiently on certain select ideas. In other words, there is no straightforward answer to the question of whether medication negatively affects creativity.

A brain that is constantly steaming ahead

Having an increased stream of thoughts isn't always unequivocally positive. Many of my ADHD patients describe constantly having 'ten different thoughts in their head' and their brain steaming ahead like an express train. During the day they struggle to concentrate, and at night they have trouble falling asleep. One of them – who happens to be exceptionally creative – described how his never-ending stream of thoughts made it practically impossible to 'be in the present moment':

'I can look at a beautiful sunset, and after three seconds I think, *OK, that was nice, but what's next?* And then new things start popping up. Others around me seem to be able to enjoy the darn sunset for several minutes,

while I can only experience that kind of harmony for a few seconds before it disappears and something else comes up.'

We are all aware that having an increased stream of thoughts has consequences, but it's telling that we just focus on the negative ones – being easily distracted and unable to stay in the moment – and forget that it can also bring an increased creative ability.

ADHD is characterised by both poor concentration and impulsivity. As you have just seen, poor concentration goes hand in hand with 'leaky attention', which is linked to increased creativity. But can poor impulsivity *also* be linked to creativity? It most certainly can! When you think about it, it's not that surprising. For even though you can improve the conditions for creativity, you can't summon a creative idea at will. It just comes to you, as an impulse. It has been shown that poor impulse control can be associated with an ability to act on creative ideas rather than simply to abandon them at the thought stage. The American psychiatrist John Ratey has even referred to creativity as 'impulsivity gone right'.

Your brain is constantly suppressing various impulses, like the impulse to pick up your phone, point out that someone is wearing an ugly tie or leave a meeting because you are bored. It's good to be able to resist both your phone and insulting someone, of course, but there is a risk that those who manage to inhibit such impulses also inhibit potentially creative thoughts. To paraphrase John Ratey, they don't allow impulsivity to 'go right'. In the same way that an increased stream of thoughts – leaky attention – can be beneficial for creativity, a lack of impulse control might also mean that you don't inhibit your creative impulses. There are always two sides to the coin.

What about hyperactivity, the third cornerstone of ADHD? What role does it play in creativity? If nothing else, it might mean having a lot of energy and being able to work for long hours. One of the most solid findings in creativity research is that creative work is often more about putting in the hours than it is about getting God-given insights from some innate talent. A person who has summed up how hyperactivity can aid in the creative process is the American rap artist will.i.am, who has ADHD: 'I've learned how to work the 'H' [hyperactivity] in ADHD to my benefit. I can work longer hours than anyone on this planet.'

Personally, I can't help but think that ADHD often means being impatient, driven and unafraid of risks, while lacking respect for authorities and traditions. If you notice that a certain routine or working method at your job isn't efficient, you don't settle for the answer 'that's how we've always done it here'. Instead, you try to find a better way. I can't think of any qualities more typical of creative individuals than being driven, sceptical, impatient and willing to take risks, while not settling for the way things are done.

Not everyone manages to bring their ideas to fruition, how-ever. After all, it's not just about generating one idea after another; you also have to do something with them. The first step, which is just as important as generating ideas, is choosing which one or ones to focus on. If you don't succeed at that, it doesn't matter how many brilliant ideas you come up with, they will remain ideas.

Selecting an idea – or a few – requires different mental functions than brainstorming. You need structure and an ability to prioritise where to focus your efforts. Once you have selected an idea, you must work steadfastly without constantly giving in to new impulses and changing your mind every few minutes. This is where many people with ADHD struggle; their ideas remain just that – ideas. Especially if they work alone.

Everyone is needed

In order to investigate how children with ADHD function in a group setting, researchers assembled several groups, each consisting of three children. The groups were composed in two ways: in some, there was one child with distinct ADHD symptoms and two children without any traits of ADHD. In the others, there were only children without ADHD symptoms. The groups were given two logical tasks to solve, and the focus was not on whether they solved the tasks correctly but on how they collaborated and interacted with each other.

It quickly became apparent that there was more turbulence in the groups where one child had ADHD symptoms. Often, that child had difficulty staying on topic and made irrelevant comments. Strangely enough, however, it turned out that these groups handled the tasks better. In nine out of the ten groups that included a child with ADHD, the children managed to solve the logical tasks correctly. No group consisting solely of children without ADHD symptoms succeeded in doing so.

As to the reasons why, we can only speculate. One possible explanation is that the child with ADHD generated new ideas that the others could choose from and actualise. Another possibility is that the child with ADHD encouraged the others to think in new ways. Simply by interacting with someone who thinks and functions differently, one is forced to think differently oneself. From a creativity standpoint, it is important that the person has the qualities we call ADHD, but if everyone in a group were to have them, things might become too chaotic. So if you have ADHD, it's important to surround yourself with people who don't – who are good at other things and can help select and develop an idea from inception to fruition. This applies to both children and adults.

ADHD and creativity go hand in hand

As you have seen earlier in the book, ADHD isn't black and white but rather a spectrum we all exist on. It has been shown that many creative individuals score highly on the ADHD spectrum. In a study of exceptionally creative children, 40 per cent of them exhibited clear signs of ADHD – meaning that they scored highly on the spectrum without having a formal diagnosis. This is another data point that indicates that the traits we associate with ADHD are closely linked to creativity.

As I've already mentioned, the psychiatrist John Ratey has described people with ADHD as having 'an itch they can never scratch'. His suggestion – which I wholeheartedly endorse – is to let that 'itch' guide you towards areas in which you can unleash your creativity. You should strive to find a niche where you can express your creative talents and where those talents are appreciated.

This doesn't necessarily mean engaging in something artistic.

Creativity is much more than painting pictures, creating music or writing screenplays or books. It can involve building something with your hands or starting and developing a business, which we'll delve into later.

Without any research to fall back on, I believe that as good a remedy as any for ADHD is engaging in something creative. Or, to be precise, this is not a remedy *for* ADHD but rather a remedy *with* ADHD – where you harness these traits and advantages rather than counteract and suppress them.

The value of daydreaming

If creativity is our most cherished cognitive ability, concentration isn't far behind. We guzzle down coffee and energy drinks to become more focused, and veritably throw diagnoses at those who struggle to concentrate. Focusing has become a virtue in today's society. Perhaps we ought to value the inability to focus a bit more highly. I believe we have become too focused on being focused.

Modern society doesn't leave much room for the daydreaming brain – the DMN. Instead, we are always walking around in executive mode, constantly swiping away any moment of daydreaming. The DMN is more or less the opposite of concentration. When you are concentrating, it slows down, but when you are unfocused and daydreaming, it kicks into gear. If you are always trying to focus, constantly planning and carrying out different tasks – first I'll do this, then that, with a quick stop at the shop and the dry-cleaner in between – you are not giving your brain space to daydream because the DMN isn't switched on. What's worse, you probably aren't allowing your brain time to be creative.

Is it possible, then, to consciously 'switch on' the DMN to become more creative? You can try to 'daydream actively', of course, but another option is to do things that don't require much thought. Boring stuff! Like vacuuming, doing the dishes or raking leaves. If the brain doesn't need to exert itself to carry out the task – after all, vacuuming doesn't require any significant mobilisation of mental resources – then the DMN will automatically switch on. And when the DMN is active, your chances of having good ideas increase. At one point or another, you have probably had a good idea pop into your head when you were doing something else entirely. Personally, I have often noticed that ideas 'pop up' when I'm doing something boring and repetitive that doesn't require much mental effort. Suddenly, the idea comes to me when I'm loading the dishwasher.

If you don't feel like doing something dull and repetitive in order to have good ideas, there is another option: make sure to have a slightly distracting background noise. Personally, I write best in a bustling café. In a quiet office behind a closed door, I find it harder to concentrate. Many people function the same way, which is why there are apps that provide just the right amount of coffee shop ambiance for people who want to work from home. What I think you are doing when you place yourself in a mildly distracting environment is increasing the activity in the DMN. You might even be making your brain a bit more like a brain with ADHD – at least when it comes to creativity. This means that increased focus isn't always the solution for every idea. To think outside the box, we must sometimes allow our brain to be as unfocused as possible. Every now and then, you have to permit yourself to daydream a little.

More creative than others

In this chapter, you have seen that there is a lot to suggest that people with ADHD are more creative than others, especially when it comes to generating new ideas. They are often better at thinking outside the box, seeing things from new angles and coming up with ideas and solutions that others fail to see. Exactly why this is, we don't know for sure, but the fact that the DMN – the 'daydreaming brain' – is more active in those with ADHD might play a significant part. Perhaps it's because of 'leaky attention', which might be the closest thing we have to an explanation of why creativity is more common in people with ADHD. Perhaps it's due to impulsivity and the fact that those with ADHD don't inhibit their stream of thoughts and ideas. Most likely, it's a combination of all these factors. Even though the precise explanation remains to be formulated, the end result is the most important thing – and we already know that many people with ADHD are more creative, especially when it comes to generating new ideas!

Is *everyone* with ADHD more creative than others? No, not everyone with ADHD performs better on creativity tests, and that's not all that surprising. It might depend on where the line has been drawn for who is invited to participate in the tests. The difficulties faced by those with severe ADHD – such as struggling with structure – can be so extensive that they completely block their creative ability. Personally, I believe that many people with ADHD might have an underutilised resource in their creativity that hasn't been allowed to flourish. For this reason, I would like to offer a few tips on what you can do to make better use of your creative abilities!

THE ADHD ADVANTAGE – CREATIVITY

Work with people who balance out your weaknesses. If you struggle with structure and focus, find someone who complements you in those areas.

Get organised – but not too organised. If you have ADHD, this might not be your strong suit, but it's necessary in order to channel your abilities. Practise and become good enough at organising.

Write down your ideas. If you have a rapid stream of ideas, there is a significant risk that you might forget them as quickly as they come to you. Make a habit of carrying pen and paper with you, or taking notes on your phone.

Force yourself to prioritise. Write down your ideas and select one or a few that you like the best.

Break down the work into several smaller tasks, where you aren't allowed to move on to the next until you have completed the one you are currently working on.

Also break down problems into smaller parts so they don't feel insurmountable and cause you to lose interest. This has to do with your brain's desire for quick rewards.

Let there be chaos if that's what works! My desk (to be honest, my entire apartment) looks like a bomb has struck when I'm writing a book. Articles, books, notebooks and Post-it notes are scattered everywhere. When I tidy up, I often notice that I forget what isn't right in front of me. It's as if I'm tidying away some of my thoughts. For instance, I can sometimes make unexpected connections when I see two books lying next to each other – 'what if you could apply this way of thinking to that area?' I have realised that I'm at my most creative in a moderately chaotic environment. If you are the same, let it be (reasonably) chaotic around you – but don't use that as an excuse not to tidy up!

CHAPTER 6

UTTERLY ENGROSSED – HYPERFOCUS

*Having ADHD makes life paradoxical. You can superfocus
sometimes, but also space out when you least mean to.*

**EDWARD HALLOWELL,
PSYCHIATRIST AND AUTHOR**

'HOW CAN MY SON have ADHD when he can sit for hours in front of the computer? He certainly has no trouble concentrating then.' Yes, it might indeed seem strange. How can someone have a condition that has concentration issues as its very foundation and still manage to sit glued to the computer or TV?

This is often known as 'hyperfocus' – the ability to be swept up in something and devote so much attention to it that you are entirely unaware of what is happening around you. This ability has – strangely enough – been found to be common among people with ADHD. I have had patients who experience hyperfocus when writing, playing an instrument, cooking or programming. It's as if time and space cease to exist. Suddenly, three or four hours have passed without them noticing.

So, how is it possible to hyperfocus while also having severe concentration issues? The answer lies in understanding the brain's attention and motivation systems. Perhaps you remember the apathetic mice that lacked dopamine and completely ignored their food? What normally happens when we see food is that our dopamine levels rise, motivating us to eat – this applies to mice and humans alike. In other words, we don't just get dopamine when we eat; we get it just by looking at food. If the food doesn't cause a significant dopamine spike, we'll ignore it, since it's not interesting enough. In order to do something, we must be motivated, and this requires a rise in the dopamine levels in our brain.

This also applies when it comes to shifting focus from one thing to another. You must feel motivated to move your attention. If you are looking at your phone and a meal is placed in front of you, the food must create a strong enough dopamine increase in your brain for you to be motivated to shift your attention from the phone to the food. If the food doesn't release enough dopamine in the reward system – perhaps because you aren't hungry or you don't like what's being served – you won't want to switch focus. You'll throw a quick glance at the plate before getting back to your phone. You won't shift your attention.

Video games provide quick rewards and continuously stimulate the dopamine system. Just think about how games tend to bombard us with an endless stream of visual and auditory stimuli. Nothing stands still, and something new happens practically every second. All this creates dopamine spikes in the brain that make you want to keep playing. This has been called 'screen sucking' – the way screens virtually suck you in.

As you have seen earlier in the book, many people with ADHD or strong traits of it have an insufficiently activated reward system. For some, a video game is the only thing that properly activates the reward system and keeps it active enough to maintain focus. The game provides a dopamine high that isn't just strong enough to encourage concentration – it's also continuous. The game continuously presents you with new stimuli.

If a child with ADHD is hyperfocused on a computer, they won't shift focus from the computer when a parent tries to get their attention. What the parent is saying doesn't create a significant dopamine spike. In the same way that we won't bother to eat the food if it doesn't raise our dopamine levels, we won't shift focus from the game to something that demands our attention if it doesn't offer the same dopamine boost. It's as if you are wearing both noise-cancelling headphones and blinders that filter out all stimuli except the game. More specifically, it's not that we hyperfocus on one thing, but that we are unable to direct our attention towards something else. It's almost like being stuck in a trance within the game, when browsing the Internet or whatever it may be.

The fact that many people with ADHD are drawn to video games has led to the misconception that gaming can cause ADHD. This is a myth – you can't get ADHD from video games. Rather, those with ADHD or strong traits of it often choose to play video games because their brain is drawn to those kinds of rapid dopamine hits. Since video games and browsing the Internet are the only things that provide enough dopamine to maintain focus, it's not surprising that individuals with ADHD are drawn to them.

Total concentration – or none at all

Of course, it's a problem if you become so completely engrossed in a video game that you play it like a person obsessed, only to suddenly realise that five hours have passed and you have forgotten to respond to important work emails or do your homework. It's easy to see that hyperfocus can be a disadvantage. But when you need to direct your attention towards something important that aligns with your long-term goals, such as work, it can also be an advantage. An entrepreneur who is completely absorbed in a task and works for hours on end can achieve wonders. A songwriter who becomes obsessed with the melody and lyrics of a song and 'resurfaces' five hours later, surprised that so much time has passed, will probably make better music than someone who gives up on composing after 30 minutes.

Being able to hyperfocus can thus be an advantage, but it's important to direct it towards something constructive. One of the most worn-out clichés is that we should try to find a job we love – something we are passionate about. Cliché or not, it's true for us all, especially for those with ADHD or strong traits of it. Many describe their concentration as either non-existent or total. Either something is extremely exciting or totally uninteresting; there is no middle ground. If this sounds like you, it's important that you try to find situations where you can achieve maximum concentration – that is, hyperfocus.

If a person with ADHD is doing something they don't enjoy, they will probably struggle to become really good at it, as their motivation will be lacking. However, if you find your passion and fully commit to it, you have every chance of becoming incredibly skilled at what you do – and utilising the advantages of your ADHD, including hyperfocus.

One of my patients with ADHD works as a chef. He has shared stories of school years riddled with failures, where he constantly felt bored and unmotivated and spent all his free time in front of the computer. Year after year of poor grades eventually made him feel worthless, not just in school but in general. His self-confidence steadily eroded as he brought home report cards that at best showed he had failed, and more often than not that he had been so absent he could not even be graded. By the age of 18, he had little hope of finding something he could be good at, let alone excel at or be passionate about. He had low expectations for his future career before it had even started.

But then, at the age of 19, he started working at a restaurant. Suddenly, he found his great passion in life – cooking – and became completely obsessed. In the restaurant kitchen, he felt like time stood still. The turbulent environment filled with constant orders where he had to keep track of many different things at once turned out to be perfect for him. 'I became completely absorbed in what I was doing and soaked up my colleagues' experience and knowledge like a sponge.'

As a result of suddenly being able to put all his energy and focus into his work instead of the computer, he became phenomenally skilled. For the first time in his life, he wasn't just as good as others at something – he was much better! 'Suddenly, I was someone. Someone others looked up to.' In hindsight, he describes how his growing self-confidence changed his life.

Today, he runs several restaurants and is one of the most prominent figures on the restaurant scene in Stockholm. 'No one in my class in upper secondary school has come close to being as successful as me,' he says proudly. And it should be noted that, despite his successes, he still struggles with ADHD. Outside of work, he finds it difficult to complete tasks, and he often has trouble concentrating in social situations that aren't work related, for which he takes medication. At the same time, he has managed to harness his ability to become utterly engrossed in a task.

Intense focus – sometimes

Another one of my patients, who works as a journalist, has shared that throughout his adult life he has had difficulty concentrating when conversing with others. Often, he loses interest after just a couple of sentences, zones out and starts thinking about something else. Socially, this is less than ideal, of course, since others perceive him as being uninterested. There is an exception, however, and that's during interviews. When the cameras are rolling and he only has a 15–20-minute window, something happens and he suddenly attains a glowing focus. 'I'm always praised for getting people to open up and share more than they initially intended,' he explains. 'It's strange how I – who have never been able to listen to anyone – can muster up such focus during an interview, even making people open up. In private, it's the opposite.'

It may seem paradoxical that he can be both socially uninterested and skilled at interviewing, but from an ADHD perspective it's not really surprising. Most likely, he has an ability to hyperfocus during interviews because he finds these situations sufficiently intense. When he shows such interest in the interviewee, they feel seen, and thus they open up and share more than they'd originally planned. Social situations, on the other hand, are not sufficiently interesting and leave him feeling bored.

Like for many others with ADHD, concentration is an either/or for this journalist. Either he has little to no concentration at all, as in social situations where he comes across as distracted and uninterested, or his concentration is total, as when he is conducting an interview. There is no middle ground.

Both the chef and the journalist can focus intensely when they are doing something that genuinely interests them. The rest of the time, focusing is a challenge. I have heard similar stories from other people with ADHD who work as programmers, car mechanics and marketing execs. They all describe facing an uphill battle in school and how, once they found their calling, they could suddenly put their hyperfocus to good use – something they had previously only experienced in front of the computer or TV. When they are truly interested, they don't just move up one extra gear but two. Suddenly, their ability to concentrate is even better than that of a person without ADHD. The individuals I'm describing haven't become successful in their professions *despite* having ADHD; they have become successful *thanks to* it.

How would the successful chef have fared in an office job? Not very well is probably an understatement. The same goes for the marketing exec, the car mechanic and the programmer. They needed to find the right place in order to excel. The importance of finding one's passion is true for everyone, but particularly so for those who have ADHD traits. If you can't find what you love doing right away, keep searching. If you still can't find it, keep searching a little longer! Sooner or later, you will succeed. The fact that you didn't give up will, to paraphrase Apple's co-founder Steve Jobs, be what made the difference. A personal reflection from all my patients with ADHD is that surprisingly many find their hyperfocus when doing something creative.

In need of constant rewards

Many individuals with ADHD can hyperfocus when something is fascinating enough and their brain receives constant rewards. So how do you get there, and what should you keep in mind in school or the workplace? There isn't a one-size-fits-all formula. The chef I mentioned earlier has one story, while the journalist and the programmer with the same diagnosis have other ones. Yet they all share a need for constant rewards. A good tip might be to break down the work into smaller segments – work for a short while, then take a break. But above all, it's crucial to identify situations and tasks that you find sufficiently interesting. In those cases, you can sit for a significantly longer time without a break.

Many people with ADHD tend to shun repetitive tasks, so it's essential to inject variety into everyday life. If your work is not very variable, perhaps it can be performed in slightly different locations? I can't help but think of how the hunter's diverse and unpredictable daily life compared to the farmer's routines. For some, routines and predictability work perfectly. For others, especially those with ADHD, they can be a nightmare.

A turbulent and noisy restaurant is the ideal environment for my patient who is a chef. In a commercial kitchen, there is always something happening. The noise level is high and new orders keep coming in, while you have to keep an eye on the food to make sure that nothing burns or goes cold. You can't postpone things for too long;

you have to act constantly. Most likely, the intensity and rapid stimuli in the restaurant create a similar effect for the chef as the interview situation does for the journalist. When life is sufficiently interesting, dopamine levels in the brain remain high, and both the chef and the journalist are able to concentrate.

In order to focus and function better, many with ADHD therefore seek out situations and environments they perceive as intense. Another option is to actively ensure that you are short on time to get something done. In other words, procrastinate until it gets urgent. It appears that many, more or less unconsciously, use procrastination as a strategy to perform at their best.

Let's say you have to write a report that is due in three weeks. By postponing the writing until you are just days away from the deadline, you force yourself to work extremely hard when it's no longer possible to delay. When the essay is due tomorrow, it suddenly becomes possible to focus, and the demand to act is so great that you also manage to perform. Constantly postponing things until the last moment can be an unconscious strategy to put oneself in situations where there is no choice – and that's when hyperfocus kicks in.

Some 30 students with ADHD were interviewed about how they managed to concentrate under pressure. When compared to their peers without the condition, it turned out that those with ADHD found it much easier to hyperfocus when the task was urgent. They could even forego eating and sleeping to get things done. In those without ADHD, the same intense focus under pressure wasn't observed.

It goes without saying that procrastination is often not a good strategy – I personally find the last few days before a book deadline to be stressful, to put it mildly. But understanding how the brain's reward system works in people with ADHD makes it clear that it's not at all strange for them to postpone tasks sometimes, and the cause isn't necessarily laziness.

A first step towards gaining control over procrastination and using it in a positive way is to learn more about it and understand why you do it. If you want to use procrastination to improve your focus, my advice is to break down tasks into smaller steps. Don't set a deadline for the entire report in two months; instead, decide which tasks should be completed two days or two hours from now. Perhaps you can even set a deadline for each chapter or page. This way, the work becomes sufficiently interesting and you won't have to stay up all night before the report is due.

No middle ground

Why do so many people with ADHD possess the ability to hyperfocus? We can only speculate, but from an evolutionary perspective it makes a lot of sense. A person with ADHD was likely a skilled hunter. Being able to muster razor-sharp focus during critical moments of the hunt must have increased their chances of catching their prey and surviving. At the same time, a hunter on the savanna needed to be easily distracted and to constantly scan their surroundings to detect the prey in the first place.

This could very well be the reason behind the paradox that people with ADHD can have both difficulty concentrating and an extraordinary ability to focus when it truly matters. As a result, their concentration is either poor or absolutely extraordinary. There is no middle ground.

THE ADHD ADVANTAGE – HYPERFOCUS

Break down bigger tasks into several steps. Are you some-one who tends to procrastinate and finds it hard to tackle a task until it's truly urgent? Try breaking down what you need to do into smaller segments. Don't view the entire essay as one task; give each chapter or page its own deadline. Don't sit in front of your books for a whole hour with a 15-minute break. Instead, read for 20 or 30 minutes, take a five-minute break and start again.

Find what you love doing. Having a job or an activity that you are passionate about is important for everyone, but for people with ADHD or strong traits of it, it's often paramount. Given that you have either a terrible or an extraordinary ability to concentrate, you need to find situations that inspire the latter. That way, your ability to become completely engrossed in a task to the point where time and space stand still can be an enormous advantage.

Consider what's important and what aligns with your long-term goals. Just as hyperfocus can lead you to spend hours on pointless activities like aimlessly browsing the Internet, it can also be an advantage – but you need to prioritise. Think about what you want to accomplish and hope to achieve in the long term. Then direct your hyperfocus towards that (which is easier said than done, of course).

Set time limits and use the alarm on your phone. Set a time limit for activities that can trigger hyperfocus but that you don't want to consume all your time, like watching TV, browsing the Internet or playing video games. Limit your gaming and TV watching to an hour or two. Set an alarm on your mobile phone, as you probably won't glance at the clock if you are very focused!

Create a sense of urgency. Mundane chores like vacuuming, doing the dishes or paying bills can sometimes feel easier if you turn them into something urgent. Postpone the vacuuming, dishes or bills until 15 minutes before your favourite TV show starts and commit to having them finished by the time it begins. But remember that not all procrastination is due to ADHD, so you can't always use it as an excuse for being delayed.

Seek out variety. If you have a brain that easily gets bored and shies away from routines, consider doing your tasks in different locations if possible.

Everyone is good at something! If you have low self-esteem because you did poorly in school, try not to let it weigh you down! It can be tricky, I know, but you will probably have other abilities that our educational system often fails to identify. If there is one thing I want you to take away from this book, it's that not everyone is suited to a theoretical classroom education, but that doesn't mean they aren't good at something else. And it certainly doesn't mean they are less intelligent.

CHAPTER 7

SHATTERING BOUNDARIES – ENTREPRENEURSHIP

My ADD brain naturally searches for better ways of doing things.
With the disorganisation, procrastination, inability to focus and
all the other bad things that come with ADD, there also come
creativity and the ability to take risks.

DAVID NEELEMAN, FOUNDER OF JETBLUE AIRWAYS

LOCATED LESS THAN TWO hours' drive north of London is the University of Cambridge. A visit to this institution invokes the weight of history; the university was founded as early as the 1200s and boasts luminaries such as Charles Darwin, Isaac Newton and Stephen Hawking among its alumni. In recent years, it's not the university itself that has garnered the most attention, however, but the surrounding area – known as Silicon Fen. Silicon Fen, boldly named after both Silicon Valley and the Fenlands in which it is located, is home to more than 2,000 companies. Most of them are dynamic start-ups springing out of research conducted at the university. Here, you'll find enterprises developing new medications, software to guard against cyberattacks, smart materials and virtual reality games. Rapidly growing high-tech companies are sprouting up like mushrooms; Silicon Fen prides itself on having a faster growth rate than China.

Despite there being a number of Silicon Fen success stories, one cannot ignore the fact that a significant portion of the companies started here ultimately fail. Behind the glamorous facade, starting and running a high-tech business is incredibly tough. The competition is fierce, and those who choose this path must be willing not only to put in an enormous amount of effort but also to recognise that the odds of success are low.

Researchers trying to understand how people make decisions had a number of entrepreneurs, all of whom had founded their own companies in Silicon Fen, take a series of psychological tests. These tests focused on decision-making – more specifically, how the participants perceived risk in various decision-making scenarios. The scenarios ranged from relatively trivial decisions like purchasing new office furniture to major decisions that could be crucial for the company's future. As a point of reference, they also tested a group of managers working in companies they hadn't founded themselves. It turned out that in decisions that weren't critical for the company, such as buying new office furniture, the entrepreneurs and managers acted similarly. These types of situations were referred to as 'cold' since the decisions weren't critical and probably didn't evoke a strong emotional reaction in the person making them.

The opposite of 'cold' decisions is the kind where the company's entire future is at stake, like when a pharmaceutical company must choose which of several potential drugs to invest millions in developing. Or when a company manufacturing smart materials considers relocating all development and production to the US in an attempt to break into the American market. Decisions of this type are not taken lightly. If all goes well, the results can be fantastic, while the wrong choice can lead to bankruptcy. Most people naturally become more emotionally engaged when a lot is at stake, and for this reason such decisions are referred to as 'hot'.

Suddenly, when testing for hot decisions, differences appeared between the entrepreneurs and the managers. When the wrong decision could have serious consequences, entrepreneurs were much more inclined to take risks, while managers usually opted for a more conservative approach. Interestingly, the entrepreneurs weren't only more risk prone, they were also more mentally flexible and better at looking at decisions from many different angles. They were also more impulsive.

This didn't mean they were willing to take reckless risks and dive headfirst into new projects, each crazier than the last, but rather that they were better at making important decisions under pressure. Managers, on the other hand, tended to freeze when faced with a significant downside and made overly cautious decisions. They were, in short, worse decision-makers when it came to 'hot' situations.

Risk-taking is a trait that's often viewed critically, but it doesn't just include reckless driving, excessive alcohol consumption or putting your savings into precarious investments. On the contrary, risk-taking and the courage to take a chance are crucial – especially in business. One of the researchers behind the study referred to the entrepreneurs' trait as 'functional impulsivity' – an ability to take calculated risks under stress; being composed enough to take a chance when an opportunity comes up, without necessarily jumping into just any crazy venture.

So what causes entrepreneurs and managers to behave so differently? Is it their genes or their environment? Apart from Silicon Valley in Northern California, it's hard to imagine a context more conducive to entrepreneurship than Silicon Fen. For someone with an idea for a new business, it's natural to take the plunge when many around you have done the same. But, setting aside the favourable environment, could there also be biological differences behind people's propensity to start companies? Could there be differences in the brain? And if so, are they hereditary? Are there 'entrepreneurial genes'?

The answer to all these questions seems to be yes! Studies of twins have shown that entrepreneurship is a propensity that is at least partly inherited. Now scientists have also begun to understand which genes are involved. When more than 1,000 entrepreneurs were examined, researchers found that a particular gene was common among them. This gene codes for a receptor for a particular substance in the brain, and you have probably figured out which one: dopamine. And this same gene has also been linked to – of course – ADHD.

Not accepting the status quo

In other words, there appears to be a genetic overlap between ADHD and entrepreneurship, which suggests it's probably not a coincidence that many entrepreneurs exhibit traits reminiscent of ADHD. I have often been struck by how many of my ADHD patients are entrepreneurs. Personality traits such as impatience, risk tolerance and high energy levels seem tailor-made for successful entrepreneurs.

As you have seen earlier in the book, a strong drive to experience new things – so-called 'novelty seeking' – has likely contributed to humanity spreading across the globe. Today, this drive is not primarily expressed as a desire to explore what lies beyond the next valley. Instead, it can take other forms. I believe entrepreneurship is one of them. Someone who 30,000 years ago would have thought, *I want to see what's on the other side of those mountains*, might today think, *I want to create a web-based payment system for small business owners*. It might sound absurd to compare these two things, but fundamentally it's a matter of not accepting the status quo and wanting to move forward instead – to keep questioning and not settle for the way things are. Breaking boundaries doesn't have to involve geographical barriers; it can also mean changing how we do things. Imagine a person who isn't the least bit impulsive, who avoids all types of risks, carefully analyses situations and turns over every conceivable stone before making a decision. Are these traits common in entrepreneurs? Not particularly.

The link between ADHD and entrepreneurship has not only been proven in genetic studies. When data from more than 20,000 individuals were examined, it turned out that the stronger their ADHD symptoms, the more likely they were to be entrepreneurs and work in businesses they had started themselves. Many people with ADHD seem to have a desire to become entrepreneurs from early on in life. In interviews with 10,000 students, it was found that the stronger their ADHD traits, the more likely they were to plan on starting a business in the future.

In the chapter 'A More Boring World', you learned that many

people with ADHD tend to get bored easily, which is probably an important reason why they decide to start their own businesses. A number of entrepreneurs, all of whom had ADHD, were interviewed for a report with the telling title 'Entrepreneurship and psychological disorders: how ADHD can be productively harnessed'. It turned out that many had gravitated towards entrepreneurship because regular jobs bored them. They chose a work situation where they could pursue their own ideas and make their own decisions.

This isn't all that strange when you think about how the brain works. If you have a reward system that runs slow, you'll likely avoid routines and predictability. You want variety – and that's exactly what an entrepreneur gets. Someone who starts a new business must initially be prepared to do everything themselves: product development, marketing, sales, accounting and office supplies procurement. Everything falls on their desk. The work is more varied but also more demanding, of course. To cope, you need energy – and that's where hyperactivity comes in handy. In fact, hyperactivity is the personality trait most strongly associated with entrepreneurship.

That they easily get bored could explain why entrepreneurs perform better in 'hot' scenarios, as I mentioned at the start of this chapter. In a critical situation, life becomes so intense that someone with ADHD can suddenly focus fully. That's when they truly excel. The same goes for multitasking – that is, doing several things at once. This also makes life sufficiently interesting.

Returning for a moment to the savanna analogy, the traits we now call ADHD were probably an advantage when hunting, allowing a person to suddenly muster phenomenal concentration and focus their energy in the right direction. And what's more similar to a critical hunting situation: a routine decision at work or a decision that's crucial for your entire business? Naturally, the latter. Many people with ADHD experience critical decisions as stimulating rather than stressful.

Entrepreneurs don't make life-or-death decisions for their companies every day, of course. However, I believe that a fast-paced environment and varied tasks can fulfil a similar function as making critical decisions. The challenging pace and workload make the environment sufficiently intense and therefore interesting.

I have also noticed that many people with ADHD or strong traits of it have the ability to see the 'big picture' and not get bogged down in details. If something is too complicated or cumbersome, they often react immediately and don't settle for the explanation 'that's the way we do it here'; instead, they ask how processes can be improved and simplified.

In addition to the desire to experience new things – novelty seeking – and the ability to see the big picture, there is another ADHD trait that can be beneficial for the entrepreneur: impulsivity. Impulsivity is about more than buying things you can't afford or saying something you'll later regret. In this context, it's more about being able to act in the face of uncertainty. It's a matter of not being too paralysed by risk, but daring to choose uncertainty over certainty – just like the entrepreneurs in Silicon Fen. And impulsivity is important for creativity. As you read in Chapter Five, many people with ADHD are more creative, especially when it comes to generating ideas. Thanks to their hyperfocus – Chapter Six – they can focus intensely on what they find sufficiently interesting.

What all of this boils down to is that some people with ADHD might be particularly well suited for entrepreneurship. At the same time, we mustn't ignore that ADHD poses its own challenges. Running a business requires being systematic, patient and structured – all things that many people with ADHD struggle with. Further, we can't automatically conclude that the strength of entrepreneurs in making 'hot' decisions applies to all people with ADHD. As with everything, there are exceptions. My advice is therefore to collaborate with people who balance out your own weaknesses, primarily looking for others who aren't like you.

The ideal career path – for you

Of course, not everyone with ADHD can or should become an entrepreneur. So, what other career paths might be suitable for those with ADHD? Naturally, one should be wary about giving specific career advice to someone they have never met, but the most crucial thing for a person with ADHD is to gravitate towards something they enjoy doing, where their personal strengths can come to the fore. A stimulating job is one that can absorb all your energy and that you can become really good at. If you find the job to be boring, it will be an enormous uphill battle to muster enough concentration and commitment to do it well.

If I were to be a bit more specific, I think individuals with ADHD should primarily choose flexible professions and positions, where they get to do a variety of tasks and one day isn't like the next. Such people are great catalysts and ensure that things get done, but many get bored easily. Finally, I think you should avoid professions with high demands on precision and a focus on details. You should try to find a dynamic role in a workplace where your talents can be put to good use and not try to fit into overly rigid systems. A profession I believe might not be a great fit for a person with ADHD is accountancy – but someone who enjoys accounting should, of course, *not* listen to me! Everyone is different, and this applies to those with ADHD, too – that's why you should follow your passion.

The super-entrepreneur

'Already back in school they thought I had ADHD, and as an adult I've been asked countless times if I have a condition,' says Martin Lorentzon.* If the name doesn't ring any bells, it's because he has effectively avoided the public eye, despite being the founder of one of the most successful tech companies of all time. In 2006, after taking his first company – Tradedoubler – public, he shifted his focus to the music industry and with his colleague, Daniel Ek, founded the music company Spotify. The company is not only one of Sweden's most acclaimed, it has also completely transformed the way we listen to music in the span of just a few years. Contrary to what one might think, however, the journey has not been a straight line, and many were sceptical when the duo launched their company. How were two guys from Sweden without any experience in the music industry supposed to succeed in doing something the global music industry had failed at?

Changing an industry that had been selling music by distributing physical records for 80 years was seen as an impossible challenge. Lorentzon recounts how they were initially ridiculed and were hardly able to secure any meetings at all. But even though it took three years of hard work before they began to see progress, he never gave

---

* Here, I must emphasise that Martin Lorentzon isn't my patient and hasn't been diagnosed with ADHD to my knowledge. He is a friend who offered to share his story when I was writing this book.

up on the belief that they would succeed. 'I knew we were right and that the CD was doomed to go obsolete sooner or later. In a digital society, you can't distribute music in the form of plastic discs.'

Lorentzon is virtually bubbling with intense energy and constantly jumps between different topics; his thoughts are often so rapid that they are difficult to keep up with. But does he have ADHD? Let's examine some of the key traits.

We'll start with hyperactivity, which can mean doing many things at once and jumping from one task to another. There is no doubt he possesses this trait. Yet, even though he has the ability to absorb and process information from multiple sources, he deliberately directs his hyperactivity towards one thing at a time and doesn't attempt to do everything simultaneously. As he explains:

> I've never had any trouble doing several things at once. On the contrary, my brain works excellently when I multitask. However, from experience I know that the results are better when I focus on one thing at a time, so I've chosen not to do multiple things in parallel. In that sense, you could say I've consciously gone against my own nature.

What about hyperfocus – does he have that ability? You don't need to speak to Lorentzon for very long to realise that he is capable of hyperfocusing like few others. When something captures his interest, he directs a burning focus towards it, especially at work.

> I can become utterly obsessed, delving into something completely, and not giving up until it works. Daniel Ek often says I'm like a badger; I bite down and won't let go until I

hear the bone snap. There's some truth to that – once I've decided on something, I don't give up.

Most people who face resistance and are misunderstood by an industry they are trying to break into might begin to question what they are doing. But for Lorentzon, it had the opposite effect.

I love being an underdog and being able to show that I'm right. That's when I perform at my best. You could probably say that I've more or less subconsciously sought out those types of situations my entire life. When I look in the rearview mirror, I can see that I've sometimes even created situations where I've had to fight from a position of disadvantage.

Lorentzon's views on risk-taking bring to mind the Cambridge entrepreneurs in 'hot' decision-making situations.

I like taking risks, but that doesn't mean I throw myself headfirst into crazy projects or that I'm completely indifferent to various risks. I often notice that others freeze and act irrationally in critical situations, whereas I can soberly assess a problem and logically weigh the pros and cons without involving too many emotions.

Lorentzon also has another trait I have observed in many people with ADHD: he has no respect whatsoever for authority figures and always focuses on the best solution, not where it's coming from. He is pragmatic and not the least bit interested in titles and office politics; what matters is the end result. Does he have many traits reminiscent of ADHD? Yes, unquestionably so. On the ADHD spectrum, where we all find ourselves, he is no doubt far above average. Can it then be said that he has ADHD? No, it cannot – and there is a simple explanation for that. To have ADHD, you must experience problems, both socially and at work. And to say that he struggles with work-related issues is utterly absurd, even though his journey hasn't always been a straight line.

Lorentzon hasn't become Sweden's most successful entrepreneur *despite* these traits, but *because of* them. He has figured out how to use his unique toolbox, but perhaps most importantly, he has learned to find people who balance out his weaknesses. 'In a personal relationship, I believe that "birds of a feather flock together", but professionally it's the opposite – there "opposites attract". I've always sought out people who complement me.'

The fact that many people suspect that Lorentzon has ADHD, no matter how well functioning and successful he is, is telling of how we view neuropsychiatric conditions in today's society. Those who have strong traits of ADHD without experiencing them as problems should neither be assessed nor treated.

THE ADHD ADVANTAGE – ENTREPRENEURSHIP

As you have seen in this chapter, a career as an entrepreneur can be a way to turn traits like restlessness and impatience into assets. If you are reading this and you have ADHD, should you consider becoming an entrepreneur? Perhaps, though naturally there are no guarantees that it will suit you. Each individual with ADHD is unique, just like everybody else. But if you are contemplating becoming an entrepreneur, here are some tips.

Find others who balance out your weaknesses. If you struggle with structure, find those who excel at it and focus on what *you* are good at. You are probably better than most at making decisions under pressure, but that doesn't mean decisions that aren't existential for the company are unimportant. If you struggle to find the motivation to make everyday decisions and engage in routine matters, make sure to work with someone who has that motivation.

Set short-term goals, too. Everyone starting a business must have a vision for where they want to be in a few years, but don't forget about short-term goals. What do I need to accomplish in an hour? What do I need to have done before I go home for the day? For people with ADHD, it's especially important to receive constant feedback. Therefore, it's not enough to only have long-term goals spanning several years. If you have an increased craving for short-term rewards, make sure to reward yourself.

Utilise your flexibility. Few entrepreneurs hit the mark right away. You have an idea of what you want to do, but along the way you might discover that the idea needs adjusting. Often, you may end up doing something entirely different. Business ideas often need to be rethought, and flexibility is a trait characteristic of many people with ADHD – so make use of it!

Focus on one thing at a time. Some people with ADHD are good at multitasking, but from an entrepreneurial perspective, it is better in my experience to concentrate on *one* idea rather than five different ones. Of course, you can perform many different tasks within the field you are pursuing, but if you try to run several completely different businesses simultaneously, there is a risk that you will do so half-heartedly.

CHAPTER 8

A NATURAL REMEDY FOR ADHD – MOVEMENT

Exercise is a small dose of Ritalin at exactly the right time.

JOHN RATEY, PSYCHIATRIST

ONE OCTOBER DAY, I was visited by a man in his mid-30s who worked as a consultant. He explained that he had been feeling well throughout most of his life except for the past six months, when he had become increasingly scattered and unfocused, without feeling sad or depressed.

When I asked him to tell me about his life, he explained that he was happily married, had a three-year-old daughter and a wide social circle. His parents were healthy and he had a well-paid job he enjoyed. 'No cause for concern either socially or professionally,' he concluded. When I enquired about his leisure activities, he mentioned that he had been a competitive middle-distance runner throughout his adult life and used to run at least ten hours a week. He also mentioned that, a few months before seeking my help, he had suffered a knee injury during a run.

The injury forced him to stop running, and that had consequences for his waistline, but his increased size was just one of the ramifications. When I asked more about his concentration issues, it turned out that they had started after his knee injury. Slowly but surely, he had become increasingly unfocused and scattered. At home, he struggled to pay the bills and keep track of paperwork. At work, the problems were even more significant, and on a few occasions he had such trouble concentrating in meetings that he recorded them to listen to again later. His colleagues noticed the change in him, and his boss asked if he was feeling unwell. He explained that he wasn't, but he didn't want to admit that he had trouble concentrating.

When he read an article about ADHD, he felt that it described him perfectly. 'It was almost eerie how the text seemed to be written about me. It described exactly how I felt.' Upon reading the article, he wanted to find out if he had ADHD, and so he sought out my help. After a couple of psychological tests and several lengthy conversations about how he had functioned earlier in life, I confirmed that he was at least partially correct in his suspicions. He scored highly on the ADHD spectrum and experienced significant problems because of it – but only when he wasn't exercising.

I explained that his regular running practice had probably functioned as a form of self-medication, keeping his symptoms at bay. Without exercise, they had resurfaced. We concluded that further screening wasn't necessary. Instead, he would try to find a new way for him to be physically active where his knee wasn't a limitation.

Whatever he chose to do, he should view it purely as concentration medicine rather than sport or exercise.

To cut a long story short, he started swimming instead, and when I met him two months later his concentration had improved significantly. By then, he had also realised that what had driven him to train so hard throughout his life had been the effect it had on his wellbeing in general and his concentration in particular.

He is far from alone. Many have experienced the wonders physical activity can do for their concentration, but what is the underlying cause? The brain's reward system is crucial for concentration, and dopamine plays a significant role here. It's believed that many people with ADHD have too little dopamine or that their reward system functions differently for other reasons.

What happens when we exercise is that we boost our dopamine levels, which primarily rise *after* working out. They seem to be at their highest after 15–60 minutes of exercise and contribute to the feeling of calm and focus that many experience after, for instance, going for a run. Personally, I often feel that life becomes clearer and crisper after playing football or going for a run. In essence, physical activity has a similar effect to ADHD medications, which also increase our dopamine levels. This means that exercise is a natural remedy for the brain – one entirely without side effects.

What many people with ADHD who exercise regularly are probably doing without realising is providing more dopamine to an inadequately activated reward system. More or less subconsciously, they feel that exercise benefits them and improves their concentration, and as a result they continue. In other words, it's hardly a coincidence that many who exercise particularly hard exhibit clear signs of ADHD. It's also not a coincidence that a long list of top athletes, such as swimmer Michael Phelps and American football star Terry Bradshaw, have openly talked about their conditions.

My 35-year-old patient had exercised his whole life before he was forced to quit and then discovered the effects running had on his concentration. One can wonder if physical activity works as a concentration booster for children, too. The answer is yes! Being physically active indeed works as a concentration booster for children, who experience improved focus after just one session. They don't even need to exercise for very long. By being physically active for just four minutes, it has been shown that children can improve their selective attention – an essential aspect of concentration.

Less impulsive and better at video games

Let's take a closer look at how physical activity affects different ADHD symptoms. In fact, the impact extends well beyond concentration issues. It also affects our impulsivity, which can be a significant problem for many. People with ADHD often say and do the first thing that pops into their head without thinking and struggle to control their impulses.

There is a psychological test that is particularly challenging for those who struggle with impulsivity. The test subject is shown the word for a colour written in another colour – for example, the word 'yellow' written in red letters. The word is only shown for a second or two, and the task is to select the colour of the letters (in this case, red) and not the word they spell (yellow). To succeed, one must restrain the impulse to simply say the word they see. This ability to control impulse, located in the brain's frontal lobe, is especially difficult for many with ADHD.

There is a simple way to help children with ADHD perform better on this test – that is, to become less impulsive – and it's to have them engage in physical activity. When children both with and without ADHD get 30 minutes of movement, they perform better on the test. Today, we know that physical activity improves what is known as our 'inhibitory control', which is the ability to restrain an impulse and not act on it. This is precisely what many people with ADHD struggle with.

Exercise makes children less impulsive and more focused. But as we all know, it can be virtually impossible to tear children away from tablets and mobile phones. So how do you motivate them to get moving? Personally, I believe that presenting facts is the best approach, but explaining that physical activity makes you better at a psychological test or improves your 'inhibitory control' doesn't sound very exciting to a 12-year-old (or an adult, for that matter). Perhaps it would be more compelling for children to hear that exercise can actually make them better at video games?

A group of children and adolescents, half of whom had ADHD and half of whom did not, were asked to test their attention using a video game where they had to perform several concentration-demanding tasks under a time limit. This wasn't a research-specific game that no one would dream of playing in their free time; it was the popular *Prince of Persia*. The specific concentration-demanding challenges in the game included a series of tasks and puzzles.

Before the experiment began, the children and adolescents were invited to play the game for a while so their performance could be assessed. Since it required concentration, as expected, those without ADHD did best. But the difference in results between those with and without ADHD could be changed with one very simple corrective: having all the participants run at high intensity for five minutes. When they resumed the game afterwards, it turned out that the children with ADHD performed just as well as those without. In other words, just a few minutes of running so significantly improved their ability to concentrate that it brought all the children to the same level.

Most likely, children's reduced impulsivity and improved concentration wouldn't just be helpful when playing a video game but also in school. The researchers behind the experiment summarised the results as follows: 'Intense exercise can improve the attention of children with ADHD and may help their school performance.'

The effects of physical activity on concentration in children and adolescents have been studied using various psychological tests, and the results clearly point towards one conclusion: everyone becomes more focused by being physically active, but those with ADHD benefit the most.

One might object that psychological tests and video games are a far cry from real-life situations. Being good at a test or a video game is one thing; the reality of school or work is another. So how does exercise affect the lives of individuals with ADHD?

This question was posed by a group of scientists who decided to ask teachers and parents of around 100 children with ADHD, who saw the children daily, to assess their concentration. The children were divided into two groups. One group got to play and be physically active for 30 minutes before school each day. The other group spent the same amount of time drawing and colouring, with the crucial distinction that they didn't get their heart rate up.

When the parents and teachers were interviewed 12 weeks later, it turned out that they perceived the children who had engaged in physical activity before school as calmer and more focused. They also had fewer mood swings, and the effects were particularly noticeable at home. Just as in the experiments involving psychological tests, *all* children who were physically active before school were perceived as having improved concentration – including those who didn't have traits of ADHD, though the effects were most pronounced in those who did.

Medication vs exercise

Does this mean that physical activity can replace medication for individuals with ADHD? Yes and no. If they engage in regular physical activity, children and adults taking medication can reduce their dose (but not without first consulting their doctor, of course), but exercise cannot entirely replace medication – it is a complement.

The first time I read about these experiments, I was surprised, and I'm probably not alone. How can it be that so many people don't know that exercise is an effective concentration booster and that people with ADHD can reduce their medication if they engage in physical activity? Almost everyone knows there are medicines that improve concentration, but why isn't it well known that physical activity has a similar effect? Fundamentally, it probably comes down to money – just as in the case of physical activity's effects on depression. It's easier to make money selling antidepressants than by spreading the message that exercise is an effective treatment for depression. And marketing ADHD medicines is more profitable than trying to encourage people to manage their symptoms by being physically active. The effects of exercise on our concentration have been surprisingly underexplored; it's only in recent years that we have begun to understand them. At the same time, astronomical sums have been invested in researching how medicines affect our ability to concentrate.

Treating the disadvantages while keeping the advantages

In the studies mentioned, researchers looked at how the ability to concentrate improved when children and adolescents with ADHD exercised. But what about the rest of us? What about those of us who struggle with concentration and have some traits of ADHD but no diagnosis? Is there research to indicate that we can also expect positive effects from exercise? Indeed, there is.

In one of the best studies on this topic, researchers examined the everyday ability to focus of more than 400 identical twins aged 17, by having their parents rate them based on factors such as concentration, hyperactivity and impulsivity. Three years later, the parents were invited to do a new rating, and it turned out that most of the adolescents had improved their concentration during that period. This wasn't surprising; after all, they had grown older. One group had improved their concentration more significantly, though, and it was the kids who were physically active in their free time. The more physically active they were, the more their concentration had improved. This even held true within twin pairs: when one twin had been more physically active than their sibling, the active twin had, on average, improved their concentration more. In these cases, the results couldn't be attributed to heredity or their environment – identical twins have virtually the same genes and have usually grown up together. That the parents perceived one sibling as having better concentration probably stemmed from differences in lifestyle – that is, how physically active they were.

What's interesting is that these young people did not have ADHD. Nevertheless, improved concentration was still observed in those who exercised regularly, and this improvement was not immediate but occurred over time – there was a three-year gap between the points of data collection.

As you have seen throughout the book, we all have traits of ADHD, which can bring both advantages and disadvantages. And it may very well be that exercise protects against the latter. ADHD is largely caused by our genes, but our environment can also play a role. Some may be born with an increased genetic risk of ADHD, but whether they actually develop it depends on the environment in which they grow up. In other words, it seems that exercise can protect those with an increased genetic risk of actually developing ADHD.

But hold on, this is supposed to be a book about the advantages of ADHD – is there a risk that you could 'exercise away' these advantages? Certainly not! ADHD is often associated with creativity, a strong drive and the ability to hyperfocus when something is genuinely exciting. There is no indication that these qualities would be negatively affected by physical activity. On the contrary, individuals with ADHD will likely become even more creative if they make sure to stay active. Exercise and physical activity are a way to treat the disadvantages of ADHD without jeopardising the advantages.

Fire up the dopamine factory

Exercise makes your dopamine levels rise and your concentration improves. Pause for a moment and consider what this means. The concentration you are experiencing right now as you read or listen to this is due to chemical reactions happening in your brain. It's caused by dopamine plugging into various receptors, and you – hopefully – perceiving these words as sufficiently interesting.

The fact that our cognitive functions, including concentration, can be boiled down to individual substances and reactions in the brain is staggering, no question. Let us therefore look at what happens in our brains if we exercise regularly for a long period.

The dopamine in our brain is formed by the substance tyrosine hydroxylase, which can be thought of as a 'dopamine factory'. The factory transforms the raw material, tyrosine, into the end product, dopamine. Experiments on rats show that this 'dopamine factory' affects behaviour. There are rats that are so hyperactive that they play in a league of their own – constantly moving and exploring their environment at a frantic pace. These rats have too little of the dopamine factory. However, when these rats are made to run on a hamster wheel, they suddenly become calm and, at the same time, their levels of tyrosine hydroxylase rise. Running thus increases the activity in the dopamine factory.

This, however, does not happen overnight; interestingly, it takes a couple of weeks of regular running before the activity in the dopamine factory increases. In other words, exercise increases dopamine levels in both the short and the long term – since dopamine levels rise immediately after a workout. At the same time, the activity in the dopamine factory increases, but this only becomes noticeable after a few weeks. The conclusion is that we have everything to gain from exercising regularly over long periods. The effects on our concentration are immediate – you may notice a difference in just a few minutes – but the truly significant benefits come from long-term, regular exercise.

So, how long should you run to achieve optimal effects in the dopamine factory? Is ten minutes enough, or do you need to keep going for a whole hour? The best results appear to be achieved by running for 30 minutes a day; according to one study it may actually be better to run for 30 minutes than for a whole hour.

EXERCISE AWAY ANXIETY AND UNEASE

Many people with ADHD struggle with anxiety, and that's not all that surprising. Naturally, concentration issues can lead to concerns about missing important things, but also about not functioning properly. It often takes a lot of energy for people with ADHD to structure their day. What others get 'for free' in terms of structure and planning, they have to work hard for, and this can, of course, lead to stress and anxiety.

For those with ADHD, exercise and physical activity target anxiety from two angles. First, they improve our concentration, which in turn reduces anxiety. Second, they have an anxiety-reducing effect that is unrelated to improved concentration, directly counteracting the anxiety itself. So, for people with ADHD who also have significant issues with anxiety and unease, it's especially important to stay active.

Boost the brain's boss

Going for a single run immediately affects dopamine levels in the brain, and the activity of tyrosine hydroxylase – the dopamine factory – increases too, with long-term benefits. In the *really* long term – over months and years – even more happens. From an ADHD perspective, the most important thing is probably the strengthening of the frontal lobe (I use the singular here, even though we have two frontal lobes – one on each hemisphere of the brain). Residing here are our most advanced cognitive functions, including the ability to direct our attention, set and follow long-term goals and not be governed by our impulses.

First, new blood vessels are formed in the frontal lobe, which not only improve the oxygen supply but also enhance the removal of waste products. Additionally, the connections between the frontal lobe and other parts of the brain are strengthened, which affects how efficiently the entire brain functions. The frontal lobe slowly shrinks in size as we age. The rate of shrinking can however be slowed down. A study that followed 20,000 American women for two decades revealed that the frontal lobe shrank more slowly in those who regularly engaged in physically activity – and 30 minutes of walking per day was enough.

So what does this have to do with ADHD? In many people with ADHD, parts of the frontal lobe are not as active. By strengthening the frontal lobe, you are bolstering an area of the brain that is central to several cognitive functions that individuals with ADHD often struggle with. This probably means striking at the very core of the issues.

Exercise is 50 ADHD medications rolled into one

As you have read previously in this book, ADHD doesn't have one and the same cause in everyone. What is expressed outwardly as concentration issues, hyperactivity and impulsivity can be attributed to various factors in the brain. An impacted reward system is undoubtedly one of the most central mechanisms, but there are others. For some with ADHD, it's believed that the thalamus, the region of the brain that filters how much sensory information reaches our consciousness, works differently. In others, it's thought to be related to the frontal lobe functioning differently.

In other words, there isn't one single 'concentration centre' in the brain; several regions are important for our ability to concentrate – and all of these can function differently in different individuals. So why am I muddying the waters by bringing this up? Well, what's interesting is that almost all mechanisms thought to contribute to ADHD improve with physical activity, regardless of the underlying cause, which can vary from person to person. Physical activity therefore isn't just *one* medication for the body and brain; it's the equivalent of fifty or a hundred.

From an evolutionary perspective, it's not surprising that exercise and physical activity make us more focused. Your brain and mine aren't much different from those of our ancestors 10,000 or even 20,000 years ago. When they went out running, it was for different reasons than ours. They certainly weren't running to trim their waistlines or improve their fitness, health or mood, but rather to hunt and escape dangers – and in such situations enhanced concentration was a survival advantage.

If you are chasing an antelope, there is no room for mistakes; it requires maximum concentration. The person who can mobilise extra concentration has the best chance of catching the antelope and, thus, the best chance of survival. In this way, evolution has honed our brains to perform at their best – at peak focus – when we are physically active. Since we basically have the same brain as our ancestors on the savanna, you and I also experience improved concentration by hitting the running track.

Today, we don't need to chase after or run away from various animals – or explore new territories, for that matter. We don't have the same reasons for being physically active as people had in the past, which is why it's crucial to ensure that we do it on our own. When a person with ADHD heads out on a run, goes to the gym or plays during breaktime, they are emulating a lifestyle they both need and were built for. Historically, those who exhibited the traits we now call ADHD were probably very physically active, perhaps because they were skilled hunters, and in this way exercise and physical activity are a way for us to get a little closer to our natural biology.

Good and bad ways to get dopamine

Physical activity increases our dopamine levels, making us more alert, focused and motivated to do things. The world feels more interesting. Is there anything else in our daily lives that has a similar effect? Well, yes: coffee is one of them! The active substance in coffee – caffeine – also increases activity in the brain's dopamine system. Most people know that caffeine has a reinvigorating effect, but they perhaps don't know that it also improves concentration.

Perhaps you have noticed the effects yourself? I certainly have. I have sat through lectures so unbelievably boring that I wondered with growing desperation how I would manage to stay awake and focused. Simply leaving wasn't a good idea, so instead I would drink copious amounts of coffee. Caffeine boosts dopamine activity in our brain and triggers the reward system, making what we are doing at that moment a little more interesting. It's a stretch to say that the lectures suddenly became thrilling, but at least they felt a bit more bearable.

Now it might sound like I have a good understanding of how I function. And even though I would like to think that is the case, the truth is that I simply felt a craving for coffee and drank it without giving it much thought. It's only afterwards, when I learned about the dopamine system and its connection to concentration and motivation, that I realised I had activated my dopamine system with caffeine to increase my motivation to pay attention.

While it remains to be proven through research, I don't think it's a coincidence that those with ADHD or strong traits of it often consume lots of coffee. But this doesn't automatically mean that everyone who drinks large amounts of coffee has ADHD, so don't go around diagnosing your colleagues with desks full of empty coffee cups! So am I trying to make you put your running shoes on the shelf and turn on the coffee-maker instead? Of course not. The point is to show what an important role dopamine plays – not just in what we call ADHD but in our behaviour in general. If we don't have enough dopamine, we will try to compensate through our behaviour.

The ultimate 'life hack'

The term 'life hack' refers to some kind of trick to help us function better in life in various ways. For people with ADHD (and to be honest, for everyone else, too), exercise is the ultimate life hack! We all have a drive to seek out things that give us more dopamine, and there are both good and bad ways of doing so. The very best way is what this chapter is all about: exercise and physical activity. It not only improves our concentration but also makes us more resilient to stress, more creative, improves our memory and makes us feel better (and it has an almost endless list of other positive effects on the body). Another way is to drink coffee (which tastes good but doesn't have very many positive side effects, of course). The absolute worst way is to use drugs.

THE ADHD ADVANTAGE – EXERCISE

How can one use exercise to manage the traits we refer to as ADHD? Every person with ADHD is different, so experiment. Do what's fun and can be made into a habit, but make sure to get your heart rate up. Ideally, aim for 20–30 minutes of activity per day, although much shorter sessions also have an effect, as you have seen in this chapter. Here are some things to consider:

The importance of everyday movement. Just four minutes of physical activity improves concentration in children, and this likely applies to adults as well. Make sure to be active several times a day by prioritising quick strolls and seizing everyday opportunities for movement. Go for a walk at lunchtime. Make the kids put down their mobile phones and go out to play at breaktime.

Opt for many short walks over one long one. If you struggle to stay focused for long periods, do your work or homework for 20 minutes, take a short five-minute walk and then work or study for another 20 minutes. This is likely better than attempting to work or study for an hour straight and then taking a 15-minute stroll.

Choose aerobic exercise over strength training, since the latter doesn't seem to have as significant an effect on concentration.

Ideally, get active in the morning. That way, your improved concentration can 'spill over' into the rest of the school or workday.

View movement as 'concentration medicine'. Find something you really enjoy doing, or at least something that feels a bit less boring. It's not about being sporty, getting a six-pack or losing weight; it's about making your brain function as well as possible. And people with ADHD need physical activity the most.

CHAPTER 9

SCHOOL – A NEW INVENTION

Any theory of education must be based on a theory
of human nature.

STEVEN PINKER, PROFESSOR OF PSYCHOLOGY

IT'S HARD TO IMAGINE a society without school. It's as if school has always existed, as natural a part of our lives as the sun rising in the morning. From a historical perspective, however, school is a recent invention. In Sweden, we have had compulsory education since 1842, and it was introduced in the UK in 1870. While that might feel like an eternity, if you imagine all of human history compressed into 24 hours – a favourite analogy of mine – then we have only had compulsory education for 15 seconds. Even if we count the schools in ancient Greece and China, which can be traced back as far as 3,000 years and had far from universal access, we have only been going to school for the last four minutes.

What about the rest of those 24 hours? What did education look like from midnight to 11.56 pm? Most likely very different compared to today. Up until 10,000 years ago, we were hunter-gatherers – or to use our analogy, we were hunter-gatherers from midnight until 11.40 pm.

During this period, knowledge was likely transmitted by observing someone else do something and then trying it yourself – learning by doing. Theoretical knowledge was probably conveyed in context. If you wanted to show a child how to track prey, how weather changes affect animal behaviour or how best to prepare a shelter for winter, you would probably demonstrate it in the environment where it would be done. Not by sitting in the same chair from 8am to 3 pm with an hour-long lunch break in between.

Let's take a closer look at how school as you and I know it developed. The foundation for modern schooling was laid during the Industrial Revolution 200 years ago. Much of what we now consider a given about school was first established back then. One example is compulsory and scheduled classes based on what year a child is born rather than their abilities. Lessons take place with students sitting behind neatly arranged desks, classes end with the ringing of a bell and several different subjects are taught in a single day by a teacher writing on a board at the front of the class.

Modern schooling is about 200 years old. But remember, our brain is the result of millions of years of evolution, and evolution usually takes a long time to make significant changes. In fact, our brain hasn't changed in 200 years – nor in 10,000, for that matter. Essentially, our brain hasn't left the savanna.

The world that shaped our brain's evolution and hence our mental capacity to learn things wasn't a world where we got our information through teacher-centred learning. It wasn't a world where we were expected to sit behind a school desk and carefully follow what a teacher is saying and writing on the board for 40 minutes, then take a 15-minute break, before starting all over again.

For many, sitting at a school desk works perfectly fine; for others, not so much. When you realise just how short a time we have had compulsory education in its current form, it's not surprising that it doesn't work for everyone. Considering how we have evolved, it's actually remarkable that it works as well as it does for so many.

We humans have an amazing ability to adapt to our surroundings. But there are limits to how much we can adapt. We differ from each other, for instance, in how we absorb knowledge. Some learn best by reading a text, others remember more when they hear information spoken, and still others need to discover knowledge more practically in order to remember it. Some can listen intently for 30–40 minutes without a problem, while others have difficulties maintaining focus for that long. One size does not fit all. From a biological perspective, it's not at all surprising that there are differences in how we learn things or that one teaching method isn't optimal for everyone. The reason that many struggle with school is just plain biology – not abnormal biology.

THE DRUG THAT CALMED 'PROBLEM' CHILDREN

Like many other medical discoveries, ADHD medications came about by accident. In the 1930s, the American physician Charles Bradley was treating a group of 'problem' children who experienced severe headaches. He prescribed Benzedrine sulphate, an amphetamine-like substance, to treat their pain.

Their headaches didn't go away, but the children became more interested in their surroundings and their emotional reactions to various events became less strong. They became calmer and more focused in school. The children also noticed the effects themselves and called the drug 'arithmetic pills', since they felt they got better at maths. Bradley was surprised that a stimulating amphetamine-like substance could actually calm the children.

In the medical world, Bradley's discovery didn't garner much attention, probably because psychoanalysis dominated during this time. In fact, it took several decades before pharmaceutical companies became interested. It wasn't until the late 1950s that the drug Ritalin was introduced to treat behavioural disorders. Initially, sales were modest, but since the second half of the 1990s they have virtually exploded.

It's important to note that Bradley believed medications are only one part of the treatment for what we now call ADHD and emphasised that environmental factors also play a part. Bradley would probably have been surprised to learn that, seven decades later, this type of drug would be used to treat more than one-tenth of all American school children. If I may speculate, I think he would have been shocked by the extent of the focus on medication and how little attention is paid to environment and lifestyle.

The Nobel laureate who climbed mountains

When the laureates of the Nobel Prize in Physics were announced in October 2016, TV experts had a hard time explaining physics laureate Michael Kosterlitz's research on how matter behaves at extreme temperatures in an accessible way. However, during the Nobel Prize ceremony, Kosterlitz revealed something much easier to comprehend: that he has ADHD and takes medication for it.

You might think that a Nobel laureate would have excelled in school, but Kosterlitz often struggled, especially with reading. He found the schoolbooks boring and meaningless. Instead, he discovered something else that captured his interest: rock climbing – and he quickly became a skilled climber. In fact, he became one of the very best in the UK, and particularly enjoyed free climbing hundreds of metres above the ground. Alongside his passion for climbing, he found another pursuit he was equally passionate about: physics. He evidently excelled at that, too.

Despite his Nobel Prize, Michael Kosterlitz is in many ways quite typical of someone with ADHD – in terms of both his strengths and his weaknesses. So, what are the advantages and disadvantages in his case? To begin with, all routines bore him, and he despises administrative tasks to such a degree that he often ignores them entirely. In these situations, he struggles tremendously with both concentration and motivation. When he feels a strong passion for something, however – such as rock climbing or research – he can suddenly focus intently, and time and space cease to exist. He enters the mental state known as hyperfocus and can perform at his very best. 'For some reason, I seem to be able to perform at the edge of my abilities to a greater extent than others,' he explained in an interview with Swedish Television's Nobel Studio in December 2016.

As you have already learned, ADHD is often linked to creativity and mental flexibility – the ability to think 'outside the box'. Conducting cutting-edge research on the innermost essence of matter requires an ability to see problems from different angles and think in new ways. No one gets the Nobel Prize for something that has already been done. Although it's difficult to prove, it is plausible that Michael Kosterlitz's creativity and mental flexibility are linked to his ADHD.

One could also view his passion for rock climbing in the context of his ADHD. For it appears that individuals with ADHD are more prone to engage in sensation-seeking behaviours like extreme sports. In these pursuits, the world becomes sufficiently interesting and they can suddenly channel their energy and attain a focus they might otherwise lack. The world becomes sufficiently interesting! Kosterlitz has shared that, at an earlier stage in his life, he dedicated all his free time to climbing and almost became addicted to it in order to function normally, like a form of self-medication. When he is climbing on cliffs hundreds of metres above the ground, his reward system likely receives the activation it otherwise lacks.

As you can see, it's not particularly surprising that a researcher of Kosterlitz's calibre might have ADHD. While grappling with the negative aspects associated with the condition, he is also able to harness its advantages and make something unique out of them. What's more, he also demonstrates that ADHD isn't a matter of intelligence. It's not about being stupid, but rather about having a brain that functions differently – and schools aren't always good at accommodating this.

Kosterlitz is a shining example of the advantages of ADHD, and the most important lesson we can learn from him is that an ADHD diagnosis should never be a limitation. There is nothing – and I mean *nothing* – you cannot accomplish just because you have ADHD or strong traits of it. Not even conducting groundbreaking research that leads to a Nobel Prize.

HOW DO ADHD MEDICATIONS WORK?

The most crucial mechanism of medications used to treat ADHD is that they raise dopamine levels in the brain by shutting down our dopamine 'vacuum'. When dopamine is released from one brain cell to another, there is a protein – the dopamine transporter – whose job it is to absorb the excess dopamine. ADHD medications get in the way of this protein and block the dopamine vacuum so that it can't absorb dopamine. As a result, dopamine levels rise. ADHD medications seem to have the biggest effect on hyperactivity, rather than concentration issues. There are also ADHD medications that work in ways other than increasing dopamine levels.

The ideal school for a person with ADHD

What kind of school would suit people with ADHD? What should teachers keep in mind? First and foremost, we must be mindful that each person with ADHD is different and there is no one-size-fits-all advice. What's more, we must also appreciate the difficulties involved in changing the school system. Smaller groups, more teachers and daily physical education aren't things that can be conjured up easily. That being said, let's reflect on what you have learned about ADHD in this book and how it might translate to the classroom.

Many individuals with ADHD seem to get bored easily, so school assignments should be made more interesting. What that means depends on the individual, of course, but a helpful example is the swimmer Michael Phelps – one of the most successful athletes of all time, with 23 Olympic gold medals to his name. When he was nine years old, he was diagnosed with ADHD due to his problems in school. He struggled with both concentration and sitting still and often disturbed his classmates. His mother, Debbie, revealed how challenging it was to motivate him to do schoolwork, until they realised they could align his learning with things that interested him. Mathematics became much more exciting when the teacher, instead of showing him the equation $200 \div 3 = ?$, asked the question: 'How long does it take to swim a 200-metre race if you swim three metres per second?' Then Phelps could suddenly see the value of learning division.

For Phelps, it was the finishing time in a swimming race that motivated him to learn mathematics. Like him, many individuals with ADHD find it easier to learn something if the task is linked to something in 'real life', so they can clearly see its usefulness.

More movement, less screen time

Mobile phones have an extraordinary capacity to activate the reward system in all of us, but especially in those with ADHD. Compared to what the teacher is writing on the board, the allure of your phone becomes almost irresistible – so remove it! Lock it away during some or all of the school day, and ensure that schoolchildren go out to play during breaktime. Since physical activity has an amazing ability to boost our concentration, this will improve conditions for learning theoretical subjects. This applies to everyone, whether they have ADHD or not, but as you have seen, it is particularly true for those with ADHD. Therefore, make sure children get moving – often.

In school, it's best to have daily physical education, preferably in the morning. That way, the increased ability to concentrate – which is partly short-lived and lasts for a couple of hours – can 'spill over' into as much of the school day as possible. Physical education in school doesn't necessarily have to be a 40-minute ordeal in the gym that requires a change of clothes. As little as 10–20 minutes of movement can work wonders for our concentration, which, as mentioned above, also means that you should make sure children put down their phones and go out to *play* at breaktime.

ADHD can mean being short-sighted in your thinking, so we should move the time horizon for tasks closer. This means breaking down school assignments into smaller tasks and setting short-term goals. Don't just plan based on what needs to be done in an hour but also in 20 minutes; not just in two weeks but also in two days, and so on. People with ADHD have a greater need for quick rewards, so clear, prompt and frequent feedback is required after completing a task. Instead of working for 45 minutes and then taking a 15-minute break, it might be better to work for 20 minutes and then take a 5-minute break, and so on.

Many people with ADHD struggle with structure and can benefit greatly from learning to divide their time into relatively short intervals. One person who has taken this to an extreme is Michael Phelps, who has shared in interviews that he breaks down his entire day from morning to evening into 15-minute blocks. He decides in advance exactly how much time he will spend eating, training and watching TV and he follows the schedule religiously. You don't have to become quite as fanatical as Phelps, of course, but he demonstrates that it's possible to deal with planning difficulties and that the end result can be truly amazing.

People with ADHD often struggle to retain information for an extended time (which involves using your working memory, such as when you keep a phone number in your mind as you dial it), and this makes it challenging for them to follow overly long instructions. Therefore, it's best not to give multi-step instructions all at once, but to break them up and provide them one at a time. This makes the instructions clear and concrete. Interestingly, our working memory has been found to be closely linked to our ability to concentrate. Research from Professor Torkel Klingberg at the Karolinska Institute in Stockholm has shown that problems associated with ADHD, including concentration issues, seem to diminish if we train our working memory.

I am not aware anyone has tried to study it, but I'm convinced that a more active approach to learning would benefit many people with ADHD. As much as possible, avoid letting them be passive spectators and try to engage them instead. Discovering knowledge on their own and not having it served to them will make a big difference for many children – and adults – who are naturally curious and prone to seeking out new experiences.

THE ADHD ADVANTAGE – IN SCHOOL

I'm no expert in pedagogy and I have the utmost respect for the challenges of changing the way things are done in schools. Based on existing ADHD research, I would still like to offer some general advice for educators. However, I must emphasise that the following should be considered overarching advice – an aspiration. Keep in mind that each person with ADHD is different, so these recommendations may not apply to everyone.

Set clear and well-defined tasks.

Give one instruction at a time, instead of several.

Provide clear and continuous feedback. People with ADHD are 'near-sighted' and need frequent and immediate feedback.

Many short breaks are better than fewer, longer ones.

Emphasise the usefulness of school assignments to make them interesting and concrete.

Include exploration and creativity in theoretical learning as much as possible. Let students discover knowledge for themselves rather than simply instructing them. Active learning is better than passive.

Try to vary the schoolwork as much as possible, using, for instance, video recordings, articles, blogs or YouTube clips. Use new technology if it makes the students more engaged.

Schedule daily physical education. Sessions don't need to last 40 minutes each time; 20 minutes of play may suffice. The key is to get the heart rate up.

Limit screen time and make kids put down their mobile phones – often.

Small classes and groups are always better for those with ADHD.

Train working memory. There are effective methods for this – for example, using a computer.

CHAPTER 10

THE EPIDEMIC OF OUR TIME

The numbers make it look like an epidemic.
Well, it's not. It's preposterous.

KEITH CONNERS, PROFESSOR EMERITUS

HAS SOMETHING HAPPENED TO the water we drink that causes us to get ADHD? You might almost think so, looking at the rapid increase in the number of people diagnosed with ADHD. The development has been explosive. In just 20 years, the percentage of children and adolescents with ADHD in the US has jumped from 3 to 11 per cent. In some states, more than 20 per cent of children have been given the diagnosis, and in Mississippi as many as 30 per cent of boys – one-third! – have been diagnosed with ADHD. Sweden is a few years behind, but it seems we are working hard to catch up. In 2022, 7.3 per cent of boys and 4.7 per cent of girls in Sweden were prescribed medication for ADHD, an increase of 400 per cent and 900 per cent, respectively, over the course of 15 years! The UK has also seen a sharp increase in the number of diagnoses between 2000 and 2018; for men aged 18–29 the increase is twenty-fold.

It's clear that money has played some part in the ballooning number of diagnoses. ADHD is big business, and ADHD medications generate a global turnover of more than $25 billion each year. Pharmaceutical companies have many reasons to aggressively market these drugs – and aggressive marketing is precisely what they have engaged in. According to *The New York Times*, all manufacturers of ADHD medications have been convicted of misleading advertising. It's hard to shake the feeling that, through cleverly designed campaigns, these companies have convinced not only doctors but also the general public that a significant portion of all children and adults have ADHD – thereby increasing the demand for their medications.

We live in a time when even the slightest mental health issue needs to be diagnosed, and preferably treated with medication. The idea that a pill can solve every mental problem is as seductive as it is naive. An indication of our newfound love for diagnoses is the sales figures for the *Diagnostic and Statistical Manual of Mental Disorders* (DSM), a diagnostic handbook used in psychiatry and published regularly since the early 1950s. If you think the title doesn't quite sound like a bestseller, you would be sorely mistaken. The latest edition made $130 million in sales. When the DSM was first published, its readers were a small group of psychologists and psychiatrists. But with each new edition, sales have steadily grown, and the DSM is now one of the world's bestselling books.

It's not difficult to read conspiracy into the fact that so many people are being diagnosed with ADHD. Personally, I think that from the healthcare system's side, it's primarily a case of misdirected goodwill. Often, we are just too quick to hand out diagnoses, and we risk mistaking curiosity and energy for a neuropsychiatric condition.

That some ADHD diagnoses must be erroneous becomes evident when we consider the fact that more children born late in the year are diagnosed. And these are not minor discrepancies. Boys born in December are almost 40 per cent more likely to be given a diagnosis than boys born in January. Is this due to some significant change in the environment between December and January suddenly causing fewer children to be born with ADHD after New Year's Eve? Of course not! It simply reflects the fact that immaturity is sometimes misdiagnosed as ADHD. For a child in primary or secondary school, a lot of development can happen in 11 months.

What's 'normal'?

What I also think might be behind the explosion in diagnoses – apart from purely economic interests – is our fundamental desire to pigeonhole both our surroundings and each other. Categorising our surroundings, not least other people, has historically helped our ancestors to survive. Which plants can I eat and which will make me sick? Which animals do I need to watch out for? Who can I trust and who should I keep at arm's length?

Our brains are therefore phenomenal at detecting patterns in what we see – for example, in someone's behaviour – and quickly sorting them into a certain box. And nowadays, these boxes largely consist of psychiatric diagnoses. 'He must have ADHD, right?' 'Isn't she a bit bipolar?' 'I think my aunt is autistic.' And so on. The more that's written about psychiatric conditions, the more you start to see them everywhere. And the more you see them, the narrower the definition becomes for what you consider 'normal'.

This is unfortunate. The spectrum of normal human behaviour is and must be allowed to remain broad, without us indiscriminately throwing around diagnoses. It would be one thing if we only used these terms for our own understanding, but the problem is that diagnoses can have real consequences. If you are told that you are 'a touch bipolar', there is a risk that you'll think there is something wrong with you that only medication can fix. The same goes for ADHD; you might think something is wrong and that certain doors in life are closed to you. But diagnoses have no intrinsic value; rather they can provide a false simplification of reality. The only reason to assign a diagnosis should be to help those who experience the most severe difficulties.

Who should be diagnosed

Considering that we all have traits of ADHD and fall somewhere on the ADHD spectrum, how many of us should be covered by this diagnosis? Should we accept that 5 per cent of us have traits of ADHD – and problems stemming from these traits – prevalent enough to result in a medical diagnosis? Or is 10 per cent a better number? Is it perhaps reasonable to assume that 20 or 30 per cent have ADHD? This is a very difficult question and one that is in essence more philosophical and political than medical. How narrowly do we want society to define what's 'normal'?

What do the experts say? In *The Lancet*, one of the world's most reputable medical journals, a group of experts write that 3 per cent of all people have ADHD. Other experts say 5 per cent, and a few

7 per cent. Among the world's leading ADHD researchers, few – if any – believe the figure should be 20 per cent. Nevertheless, that's how many children and young people have been diagnosed with ADHD in some US states.

Let's combine all these ingredients: our basic drive to categorise, a diagnosis that cannot be clearly delimited and that many have traits of, medications that improve many people's concentration, and strong commercial interests. Add to this that there may also be others with an interest in diagnoses being given, such as schools, which may receive additional resources for pupils with ADHD. Looking at the big picture, the inevitable result quickly becomes clear: more diagnoses and more medication. And that's precisely what we are seeing.

But how long will the number of diagnoses continue to rise? There is reason to believe this trend will persist. As you have seen, the fact that we all fall somewhere on the ADHD spectrum is no stranger than the fact that we are all different heights. Let's make a historical comparison between concentration and height. In the mid-nineteenth century, the average height of a Swedish man was 1.67m; today it's 1.81m. (The increased average height is believed to be due to factors like better nutrition and fewer childhood infections.) A man who measured 1.77m in the mid-nineteenth century would probably have been considered tall, but that would hardly be true today. The same goes for concentration: 150 years ago, the demands on concentration were lower and there were plenty of jobs for those with concentration difficulties – such as physical labour on a farm or in a factory. Today, those types of jobs have been all but phased out.

An increasingly complex society places greater and greater

demands on our cognitive functions, which means that more and more people fall below the level of concentration required in the job market. There are many reasons to believe this trend will continue. Rapid technological advances in robotics and artificial intelligence will make our lives easier, but they will also automate jobs and place ever-greater cognitive demands on the remaining ones. This could mean that more and more people will struggle to find work and begin to wonder what is wrong with them. To wonder what is wrong with oneself in today's society is to ask if one has a psychiatric condition.

Medication for everyone?

In a live TV interview, I warned that Sweden should avoid becoming like the US – where more than one in ten children have been diagnosed with ADHD. I was subsequently asked why it would be a bad thing for so many to receive a diagnosis. I must admit the question took me aback; it seems rather obvious that we shouldn't make diagnoses too liberally. Yet the question is justified. What does it *really* matter if lots of people are diagnosed with ADHD?

In practice, an ADHD diagnosis often results in being prescribed medication. So let's consider what would happen if, for instance, we prescribed medication to all school children. Would it have any effect on the concentration of those who don't have significant issues? Probably – those who don't rank highly on the ADHD spectrum would likely also become more alert, focused and have better concentration, functioning better in school. This can be gleaned from the fact that one in six American college students has at some point bought ADHD medication illegally to help them cram for an exam. One student described his ADHD medication in vivid language as 'get-shit-done pills'.

But if the medication works and enhances concentration in so many, why not allow anyone to buy it over the counter at the pharmacy or supermarket, just like regular pain relief? There are some reasons why this is a bad idea. One is that the medication can have serious side effects, such as causing severe anxiety in some people. Some experience reduced appetite, disrupted sleep and a changing mood. In the long term – and by that I mean decades – there are cardiologists who have warned that cardiac health could be negatively affected.

Medicine is fundamentally about weighing pros against cons. And it's not only a matter of balancing the benefits of treatment against the risks; it also requires us to consider the risks of *not* providing treatment. That's why doctors are normally – or at least should be – cautious about making overly categorical statements. If you give the same advice to 100 people, it may be correct for 99 of them but catastrophic for the last one. This is why doctors want to gather as much information as possible in each individual case and carefully weigh up the pros and cons before making a decision.

Side effects and unknown long-term risks are two major reasons why we should be cautious about prescribing ADHD medication too readily. At the same time, we must consider the consequences of not providing medication to those who have difficulties. If a child cannot function in school without medication, the cost is very high for that child.

When weighing the pros against the cons, I think it boils down to the benefits of medication outweighing the risks for those with the most severe issues. They should receive a diagnosis and, if necessary, be offered medication. For people with only minor problems – and that group is large, given that we all fall somewhere on the ADHD spectrum – the risks outweigh the benefits. In such cases, it's best to wait or at least consider medication as a last resort after trying everything else.

So, how many people actually have ADHD? I think it's reasonable to estimate that around 5 per cent of the population has ADHD, and half of them need medication. This would mean that just under 3 per cent of all children should receive medication – on average, one in every class.

When medication works wonders

'Sorry I'm late,' a 46-year-old female patient gasps as she dashes into my office, 25 minutes late, after running from the parking lot.

'No problem. What can I do for you?' I reply.

The woman quickly takes a seat and says, still catching her breath, 'I think I have ADHD, and I need help.'

Yet another person who has googled 'ADHD' and decided to self-diagnose, I think to myself. 'Tell me, what makes you think that?'

As she begins to chronicle her life story, it doesn't take long for me to start feeling guilty about my initial reaction.

'School really wasn't for me, right from first grade. I would focus on just about anything except what the teacher was writing on the board. At the slightest distraction, I'd lose focus and get bored. I was disruptive and misbehaved all the time and could never sit still. So I was put in a special-needs class already in primary school.'

Yet around the same time, she also began to show a talent for basketball, and on the court she managed to channel the energy that caused her such trouble in the classroom. She soon started playing for the local team and quickly became their star player. Her sporting success eventually led her to play at an elite level, and at the age of 20 she got a scholarship and the opportunity to play college basketball in the US.

'Right there, my life could have taken a different turn. But instead of focusing on my big chance – basketball – I quickly fell in with the wrong crowd and started using drugs. First it was hash, and eventually amphetamines and cocaine. After a couple of years, when I got caught for drug possession, it ended in a prison sentence,' she explained.

Her two years in a brutal American women's prison were hellish. She was harassed by other inmates and severely beaten on several occasions. It would have broken most people, but after her release, she quickly shrugged off that period in her life and was determined to move forward. It didn't take her long to get back on her feet. Through an Indian rug supplier, she began importing and selling rugs, starting small out of her home, but gradually growing the business – and soon it was booming. She found a space and opened a shop; when that did well, she opened another one. The income from the rug sales allowed her to buy both a bigger apartment and a car. She also fell in love, and just like that her life was back on track.

But after a couple of happy years, her life took another turn. When it came to light that her boyfriend also had a drug problem, she relapsed. As her drug use escalated, she began neglecting her work and the rug company went bankrupt. At the age of 29, she was homeless and mired in debt.

Before turning 30, she had experienced more turbulence than

most do in a lifetime. And this wild rollercoaster ride continued in the years that followed. In fact, her entire life had been utter chaos.

She was driven by constant impatience, which often had disastrous consequences, but which also served as a powerful engine and occasionally resulted in relatively big successes in her career. 'It's as if I have a rocket engine inside me, constantly propelling me in all sorts of directions. Sometimes towards what's good, but all too often towards what's bad,' she explained.

As she told her story, I couldn't help but feel fascinated by her incredible ability to get up after every setback and keep fighting. If I had experienced even half of what she had been through, I would probably have been so beaten down that I could hardly get out of bed in the morning. But it wasn't just her story that was remarkable; her entire demeanour was odd. She spoke intensely and engagingly, but far from clearly. There was no straight timeline to her story; she made constant digressions. Sometimes she spoke so quickly that I had to ask her to slow down so I could keep up. Moreover, her right leg shook restlessly throughout our conversation, and when a nurse knocked on the door to give me some referrals, she twitched so violently it was almost comical.

So what happened next? Well, after several psychological tests and interviews, I diagnosed her with ADHD and prescribed medication. I asked her to come back two weeks later to see how it was working, and when I arrived at work that morning, there was someone in the waiting room I didn't initially recognise. I walked into my office, turned on my computer and saw that the 46-year-old woman was my first patient of the day. Clearly, she hadn't arrived yet. *She's probably running late again*, I thought and started going through my emails.

Ten minutes later, there was a knock on the door and there she stood – the person in the waiting room I had rushed past without recognising. In my defence, it wasn't so strange that I didn't realise it was her. It wasn't just her clothes and hairstyle that had changed, but her whole demeanour and body language. She exuded a sense of calm and harmony that was like night and day compared to the nervous, rushed person I had met two weeks earlier.

'I actually didn't recognise you. How are you doing, and how has it been?' I asked, feeling slightly embarrassed.

'Honestly, it's amazing. I've never felt so good. For the first time in my life, I understand how you're supposed to feel and be. It's as if the background noise in my head has suddenly been switched off. I can focus. I hear what other people are saying. I can be present in a way I've never been able to before. I'm not somewhere else in my thoughts. My constant anxiety is gone, and my inner rocket engine has slowed down. The medication you gave me has worked wonders.'

The change was so striking, I have never seen anything like it in all my years as a psychiatrist. It was amazing to see that we had found the right treatment for the mental disability she had been struggling with her entire life. In my profession, these are the moments you live for.

Why am I sharing this story about my female patient? Well, because many like her struggle with enormous problems in life due to the traits we call ADHD. They suffer greatly from both an innate inability to concentrate and an impulsivity that is simply impossible to control. For them, an ADHD diagnosis and medication can be lifesaving.

Does she fit the profile of all people with ADHD? And does medication have the same positive effects on everyone? No, of course not. On a ten-point ADHD scale, she gets a perfect score. In fact, she probably scores 99 or 100 on a 100-point scale. There is no doubt whatsoever that she is well on the ADHD side of the grey area between normal concentration issues and ADHD that I have described in this book.

I don't want to downplay the seriousness of ADHD in any way or rail against medication. For the right person, it may be the only thing that works – like the woman I just told you about. But it doesn't mean that 10 per cent of the population should be medicated. We need to focus on the right individuals – the ones with the most severe issues – and medication should be a last resort, not the first. If too many people are diagnosed, ADHD may become trivialised, and there is a risk that the people with the most severe problems won't get the help they need. The danger is that people with difficulties on the same level as my patient will be told, 'Oh, you have ADHD too – get in the line that consists of 10 per cent of the population.'

There is another reason why I mention her specifically. She is a shining example of a person who keeps going despite setback after setback. She simply refuses to be crushed. To my knowledge, there hasn't been any research on ADHD and the ability to shrug off one's failures, but after meeting hundreds of patients with similar traits, I find it hard to believe it's a coincidence. Many people with ADHD don't dwell on problems and difficulties; instead, they look forward and refuse to be disheartened. They move on.

No blank slates

A large number of politicians, thinkers and psychologists have stated that humans are born as blank slates and can develop just about any personality traits and characteristics. It's a nice idea, but today we know that's not true. Our personality is not only influenced by our environment but also by heredity – that is, our genes.

The human brain is incredibly malleable, and how we function mentally is largely determined by our lifestyle. Yet from the moment we are born, we have different predispositions when it comes to various psychological traits. Today, we know that our personality is influenced in part by the genes we are born with, and scientists are currently making significant strides in explaining which genes underlie our various personality traits. Five of these traits are considered so fundamental that they are referred to as the 'big five' in psychological research. Among these is the trait of openness: being curious, imaginative and open to new experiences and ideas. Both you and I have varying degrees of openness, and we also have more or less of the other four traits, which are extroversion, conscientiousness, neuroticism and agreeableness.

When scientists have examined the genetics behind personality, it turns out that all of the big five can be linked to different genes. There are genes that contribute to making us extroverted and genes that promote conscientiousness. Other genes determine how neurotic we are, and so on.

Genes account for about half of how much we have of each of the big five personality traits; the rest depends on our environment. Interestingly, there seems to be a genetic overlap between different personality traits and psychiatric conditions. Several of the genes that affect how neurotic a person is can also be linked to the risk of developing depression. Most likely, this overlap contributes to an increased risk of depression in individuals who are neurotic. So what does this have to do with the advantages of ADHD? Well, many of the genes associated with the personality trait of openness are also linked to ADHD. Genes that contribute to our openness to new experiences, curiosity, adventurousness, imagination, creativity and independence are thus largely the same genes that influence whether we have ADHD. Personally, I can't think of any other personality traits that are more positive than this – if any.

Genes explain our personality

Enormous advances have been made in genetic research. Today, we not only study which genes influence the risk of cancer or cardiovascular disease, but also which genes affect personality traits like the big five, whether we would rather run or walk up stairs (no, I'm not kidding!) and how we behave in social situations. Genetic research has taken the leap from understanding what makes us sick to explaining our personality.

This growing body of knowledge is undoubtedly fascinating. At the same time, there is a risk that we will continue to view genes as factors that lead to either sickness or health, even as we learn more about the genetics behind our personality traits. That would be unfortunate. When it comes to personality traits, there is usually no right or wrong, no such thing as sick or healthy. Certain psychological characteristics and personality traits can cause suffering, but it's important that genetic research doesn't lead us to narrow the definition of what's considered 'normal'.

The same goes for our increased ability to image the brain, where progress has been rapid. Just a couple of decades ago, the most advanced technology could – at best – provide low-resolution images of brain tumours or bleeds. Today, we can study the brain with milli-metre precision without risk to the person being examined. Advanced brain scans can now generate 1,000 gigabytes of data from a single person. This development is amazing, but we must be careful not to automatically label variations in the brain between different people as either sick or healthy, because this much is certain: at that level of detail, variations will be found!

An example of this is when the media made a big fuss about parts of the brain being smaller in individuals with ADHD. It's true that there are some differences in size between those with ADHD and those without. The differences are very small, however. And what's more, they can't automatically be translated into how the brain func-tions. What the study does show, though, is that ADHD isn't a made-up diagnosis or a result of one's upbringing; it's actually a matter of biological differences in the brain. Yet that doesn't mean we can draw a clear line between what's normal and what's not.

Reality vs research

Much of the research I have presented in this book is the result of studies on children and adults with ADHD. They have been care-fully examined to ensure that their concentration issues and impulsivity are not due to factors such as a chaotic classroom or something else in their environment. Researchers want to make sure that those people included in the studies really do have ADHD.

Is the same level of scrutiny applied when diagnosing ADHD in practice? It's my impression that it often is, but far from always. Sometimes doctors give an incorrect diagnosis, and sometimes factors unrelated to what's happening in a person's head – such as a disruptive study environment – are misinterpreted. Another example is that more children born late in the year get this diagnosis because immaturity is mistaken for ADHD. And just because a series of research studies has shown that there appear to be differences in the brain's reward system in a significant percentage of those with ADHD, that doesn't mean 30 per cent of all boys in Mississippi have such differences!

Those with an ADHD diagnosis are, in practice, a highly heterogeneous group. This isn't only because several different biological mechanisms can lead to ADHD symptoms, but also because some may have been diagnosed with ADHD when their symptoms actually stem from something else. An important conclusion for anyone with an ADHD diagnosis is not to believe that everything they read about ADHD applies to them. Humans are much more complex than can be boiled down to a single diagnosis. This also means that I and my colleagues who give out diagnoses need to become better at ensuring that those who receive an ADHD diagnosis truly have the condition – and that there isn't something else causing similar difficulties.

Brains are supposed to be different

Humans are social animals and the brain is wired for cooperation, even though it may not always seem like it in our individualistic era. We fight to outdo each other with the most spectacular food and holiday photos on social media, but fundamentally we are still social creatures, and the most important thing for the group is that everyone is *not* the same. For humans and other species alike, it's crucial that many different traits are represented.

When some of the remaining hunter-gatherer societies on earth have been studied, it turns out that some tribal members have the DRD4-7R gene – that is, the ADHD gene. Not all members have it, even though it seems to offer advantages in the environment they live in. The same pattern can be observed worldwide, with some people having the gene and some not. It's probably not a coincidence, since not everyone can be impulsive and hyperactive. For a society to function, there must also be individuals who are patient, who plan for the long term and who don't follow their every impulse.

On an emotional level, one might find uniformity repulsive, but the fact is that biologically it's clear that we are *supposed* to be different. The term 'neurodiversity' was coined in the 1990s and refers to the idea that there is not one singular way for the brain to develop and function 'normally'. We need to change our perspective on ADHD and autism – from pathologising and seeing them as medical conditions associated with a disorder, to seeing them as normal variations in human behaviour. Everyone knows that we are different heights and have different hair colour, and we don't consider that abnormal; the same should apply to our personalities. The traits we label as ADHD – and autism, too, for that matter – are nothing more than variations in human personalities.

This doesn't mean I want to downplay the challenges. Those who face significant problems in life due to ADHD need help, of course, just like those who struggle with anxiety or depression do.

However, just as we shouldn't rush to diagnose and medicate the slightest period of worry or sadness, we also shouldn't do so for the slightest hint of ADHD. And getting help can mean much more than simply being prescribed medication. It's no more complicated than that.

It's society that needs to change

As you read in Chapter 4, swans that don't like city life fly to the countryside. This results in rural swans having certain genetic differences compared to those living in urban parks. The conclusion is simple: swans end up in the environment that suits them best. However, this system only works if swans that are not suited to a particular environment can take off and choose a different home. The problem is that you can't exactly 'take off' from today's society. If you are a child in school with traits that worked well when we were hunters on the savanna, you can't just move out into the woods and live off the land. Instead, there is a risk that you'll end up with poor grades and shattered self-confidence.

At its core, it's a matter of how receptive and well equipped our society is to accommodate different personality traits. If I may paint with very broad strokes, I would say that we aren't very good at this and instead try to squeeze everyone into a 'normal' box. If 10 per cent of all children need a diagnosis and amphetamine-like medication to cope with school, it's not 10 per cent of children who are the problem – it's our school system. To quote the American paediatrician Michael Anderson: 'We've decided as a society that it's too expensive to modify the kid's environment. So we have to modify the kid.'

The ADHD advantage

As you have seen in this book, the brain's reward system functions like an engine that drives us towards different behaviours, and for millions of years evolution has fine-tuned this engine with a single purpose: to make us engage in activities that ensure our survival and reproduction. It's a system that is utterly ingenious, yet it evolved for a different world than the one you and I live in now. If we imagine 50,000 of your ancestors gathered in a big room, the reward system has evolved to benefit 49,500 of them – the ones who lived up until 10,000 years ago – rather than you and me.

We have brought our powerful reward system into the modern world, which in many respects doesn't chime with our biology. Our transition to modern society has happened rapidly, in just a few hundred years, and the pace of change is increasing with every decade. The time we live in is entirely unique, not only in the history of our species, but in that of all species.

One example of this is the way our reward system floods us with extra dopamine when we consume calorie-rich foods. Most would probably agree that the tastier a dish is, the more calories you can be sure it contains. In fact, your dopamine levels rise if you only look at calorie-rich foods, so that you'll be motivated to eat them. The reward system tells you: 'Devour that bag of crisps immediately!' This mechanism worked well in a world with a scarcity of calories, where it motivated our ancestors to eat every little calorie-rich berry they could find. Thanks to this, they had energy reserves to draw from if there was no food the next day. But in a world full of fast-food restaurants, this mechanism doesn't serve us well at all when it makes us gulp down all the calories we come across as protection against a famine that never comes.

Today, more people die from *overeating* than from starvation, and it's precisely because of this. The craving for calories that evolution built into us over millions of years in a calorie-starved world has been brought into our modern society where calories are everywhere and practically free. With this in mind, it shouldn't come as a surprise that more than 2 billion people in the world are overweight or obese, and that half of humanity is expected to be by 2035.

So where does ADHD come into all of this? Well, our reward system doesn't just guide us towards certain behaviours; it's also crucial for our concentration. Since we struggle to concentrate on things that don't generate sufficient activity in the system, we constantly scan our surroundings for something that can activate it. This used to increase our chances of detecting both dangers and prey in the world of our ancestors. But in a classroom or open-plan office, this constant scanning and the impulse to act quickly can suddenly become a hindrance.

I think we can understand ADHD much better if we are aware of what I have just described – though it might be cold comfort for students with poor grades to hear that they would have been well suited to life on the savanna 10,000 years ago. And that's where the topic of this book comes into play. ADHD has not only brought advantages historically, but it still does so today.

As you have seen in this book, we all have traits of ADHD – some more than others. For most people with strong traits and who rank highly on the spectrum, I think we should start by looking at the environment before resorting to diagnoses and medication. Is there something we could change in the classroom, at work or at home to help them manage the difficulties that ADHD can involve? Both the individual with traits of ADHD and the people around them should ask themselves what *advantages* ADHD can bring. The best way to answer this question is to learn more about what ADHD is. Why do I struggle with certain things, and why am I good at others? How can I make the best use of my abilities and strengths in life? Don't try to force a square peg into a round hole; instead, find *your* advantages with ADHD. I hope this book has helped you understand them better.

AFTERWORD

Let's not rush to medicalize . . . curiosity, energy and novelty-seeking; in the right environment, these traits are not a disability, and can be a real asset.

RICHARD A. FRIEDMAN, PROFESSOR OF PSYCHIATRY

FOR EVERY COMPLEX QUESTION, there is a simple, clear and straightforward answer – that's wrong. ADHD is one such complex question. What is ADHD, *really?* Is it a disability or a superpower? Can it help me in life or just get in the way? The answer is that ADHD can be all these things to different people. ADHD does not have a brief answer; instead, it requires that we view it from multiple angles. In this book, I have chosen to present one perspective – that ADHD can actually serve as an advantage.

The fact that psychiatric diagnoses are so focused on problems is a natural consequence of psychiatry being a branch of medicine. In medicine, diseases are the primary focus. A cardiologist is normally more interested in how to treat a heart attack than in strengthening an already healthy heart. A surgeon cares more about how appendicitis develops than the physiology of a healthy appendix. There is nothing strange about that, but the problem is that psychiatry works the same way. Researchers focus on issues resulting from psychiatric conditions like autism and ADHD and too often forget that they can also bring advantages. ADHD isn't like a heart attack or appendicitis – bad no matter how you slice it. It's a coin with two sides, though usually we only care about one.

Being easily distracted can also mean that you are more creative. Being hyperactive means you have boundless energy. Having trouble concentrating on everyday tasks might, paradoxically, mean that you have an incredible ability to focus when you find something that truly interests you.

I have met countless patients with ADHD and have seen many of them do well in life. Those who have managed to turn the traits associated with the condition into something positive have had one thing in common: they have all had insight into both their weaknesses and their strengths, and have learned to harness the latter. And if they haven't had this insight themselves, someone around them – be it a parent, teacher or partner – has understood that they have both difficulties and a unique toolbox at the same time. This is precisely why I have written this book, in the hope that more people will come to see themselves as unique rather than broken.

There is yet another reason to be careful about comparing ADHD to other medical conditions. Heart attacks and appendicitis don't pay any attention to the labels we give them – but the brain does. If you are told that you have a psychiatric condition like ADHD, it can turn into a self-fulfilling prophecy.

Am I alone in pointing out that ADHD may have been an advantage historically? Far from it. The American psychotherapist and author Thom Hartmann presented this idea as early as the 1980s. At the time, many were sceptical and dismissed his arguments as wild speculation. Back then, ADHD was seen as a brain injury, and the term MBD was still being used. Today, the situation is different. The research I have presented in this book provides support for the idea that ADHD has been – and can still be – an advantage.

Finally, this is a popular science book, and as such I had to make certain simplifications for the sake of readability. In the Bibliography I have therefore compiled all the studies this book is based on, so that those who want to know more can go straight to the source.

Three people left us while I was writing this book, and it has made my world and many others' considerably emptier. You will forever be sorely missed.

Johannes Croner (1972–2017)

You weren't just the best doctor and surgeon anyone could imagine, you were also the most thoughtful friend. I'm eternally grateful for all our travels and the memories we made together, all around the world. You will always be my role model, both professionally and personally, and you will always be deeply missed. I'm proud and thankful to have been your colleague, and even prouder and more thankful to have been your friend.

Tomas Linnala (1965–2017)

Thank you for teaching me to write when I took a side job at Dagens Industri to fund my medical studies. Without you, there probably wouldn't have been any books. Your broad intellect traversed many areas, and you were always a great source of inspiration to me. I'm so grateful for all our conversations and for your unwavering helpfulness and willingness to spare your time.

Hans Rosling (1948–2017)

On several occasions, I had the great privilege of discussing medicine, research and global health with you, and I learned more from each conversation than I could glean from any book. You taught me the value of communicating science and provided invaluable advice on how to do so. Thank you for having been – and always continuing to be – such a role model.

GLOSSARY

DEFAULT MODE NETWORK (DMN) A collection of areas in the brain that form a network that is activated when we are not actively engaged in a task – for example, when we are daydreaming. The DMN is believed to be important for creativity.

DOPAMINE A substance that regulates our feelings of wellbeing and particularly our motivation, rewards and 'drive'. Dopamine is found in the reward centre and in the frontal lobe, where it is important for inhibiting impulses. Dopamine also plays a role in our physical movements, in a region of the brain called the basal ganglia.

DOPAMINE TRANSPORTER A substance that reabsorbs dopamine from the gap between two brain cells, thereby lowering dopamine levels between the cells. It acts like a kind of dopamine 'vacuum'. Many medications for ADHD function by blocking the dopamine transporter, which means the vacuum can't be quite as active, consequently increasing dopamine levels.

DRD4 (DOPAMINE RECEPTOR D4) There are several receptors that dopamine binds to. One of them, number 4, is found in the frontal lobe and in the brain's reward centre. There are several different variants of the DRD4 gene, and each person has the variant they were born with. One of the variants, DRD4-7R, has been linked to curiosity and so-called novelty seeking, and has been found to be more common in people with ADHD. Approximately 20 per cent of all people on earth are born with DRD4-7R.

FRONTAL LOBE The part of the brain that sits behind the forehead; the seat of logical and abstract thinking, as well as our ability to regulate our emotions. The frontal lobe is the most advanced part of the brain.

MUTATION A change in a cell's genetic material (DNA or RNA) that can result from a random error that occurs during cell division or from exposure to toxins or radiation. Mutations can make cells function better or worse. If a mutation occurs in a sex cell – a sperm or an egg – it can be passed on to the next generation.

NEURON A brain cell.

NUCLEUS ACCUMBENS A small part of the brain that is important for our reward system and for driving our behaviour. Dopamine is a crucial substance in the nucleus accumbens, and when dopamine levels rise we feel good.

THALAMUS A central area in the brain through which a large portion of the information from our sensory organs (ears, eyes, etc.) passes on its way up to the cortex and consciousness.

TYROSINE HYDROXYLASE An enzyme that synthesises dopamine. It can be thought of as a 'dopamine factory' that converts raw material (tyrosine) into the end product: dopamine.

BIBLIOGRAPHY

1. Two Sides of the Same Coin

Gallo, E.F. and Posner, J. 'Moving towards causality in attention-deficit hyper-activity disorder: overview of neural and genetic mechanisms.' *Lancet Psychiatry* 3; 6 (2016): 555–67. DOI:10.1016/S2215-0366(16)00096-1.

Geschwind, D.H. and Flint, J. 'Genetics and genomics of psychiatric disease.' *Science* 349; 6255 (2015): 1489–94. DOI:0.1126/science.aaa8954.

Hoogman, M. et al. 'Subcortical brain volume differences in participants with attention deficit hyperactivity disorder in children and adults: a cross-sectional mega-analysis.' *Lancet Psychiatry* 4; 4 (2017): 310–19. DOI:10.1016/S2215-0366(17)30049-4.

Lubke, G.H. et al. 'Maternal ratings of attention problems in ADHD: evidence for the existence of a continuum.' *Journal of the American Academy of Child & Adolescent Psychiatry* 48; 11(2009): 1085–93. DOI:10.1097/CHI.0b013 e3181ba3dbb.

2. A More Boring World

Asghari, V. et al. 'Modulation of intracellular cyclic AMP levels by different human dopamine D4 receptor variants.' *Journal of Neurochemistry* 65; 3 (1995): 1157–65. DOI:10.1046/j.1471-4159.1995.65031157.x.

Dalley, J.W. et al. 'Impulsivity, compulsivity, and top-down cognitive control.' *Neuron* 69; 4 (2011): 680–94. DOI:10.1016/j.neuron.2011.01.020.

Dalley, J.W. et al., 'Nucleus accumbens D2/3 receptors predict trait impulsivity and cocaine reinforcement', *Science* 315:5816 (2007), 1267–70. DOI: 10.1126/science.1137073.

Dobbs, D. 'Restless genes.' *National Geographic* (Jan 2013).

Gizer, I.R. et al. 'Candidate gene studies of ADHD: a meta-analytic review.' *Human Genetics* 126; 1 (2009): 51–90. DOI:10.1007/s00439-009-0694-x.

Li, D. et al. 'Meta-analysis shows significant association between dopamine system genes and attention deficit hyperactivity disorder (ADHD).' *Human Molecular Genetics* 15; 14 (2006): 2276–84. DOI:10.1093/hmg/ddl152.

Li, Z. et al. 'Molecular genetic studies of ADHD and its candidate genes: a review.' *Psychiatry Research* 219; 1 (2014): 10–24. DOI:10.1016/j.psychres.2014.05.005.

Muglia, P. et al. 'Adult attention deficit hyperactivity disorder and the dopamine D4 receptor gene.' *American Journal of Medical Genetics* 96; 3 (2000): 273–7. DOI:10.1002/1096-8628(20000612)96:3<273::aid-ajmg7>3.0.co;2-z.

Plichta, M.M. et al. 'Neural hyporesponsiveness and hyperresponsiveness during immediate and delayed reward processing in adult attention-deficit/hyperactivity disorder.' *Biological Psychiatry* 65; 1 (2009): 7–14. DOI:10.1016/j.biopsych.2008.07.008.

Ridley, M., *The Red Queen: Sex and the Evolution of Human Nature* (London, Penguin Books, 1994).

Scheres, A. et al. 'Ventral striatal hyporesponsiveness during reward anticipation in attention-deficit/hyperactivity disorder.' *Biological Psychiatry* 61; 5 (2007): 720–4. DOI:10.1016/j.biopsych.2006.04.042.

Schou Andreassen, C. et al. 'The relationship between addictive use of social media and video games and symptoms of psychiatric disorders: a large-scale cross-sectional study.' *Psychology of Addictive Behaviors* 30; 2 (2016): 252–62. DOI:10.1037/adb0000160.

Sharp, S.I. et al. 'Genetics of attention-deficit hyperactivity disorder (ADHD).' *Neuropharmacology* 57; 7–8 (2009): 590–600. DOI:10.1016/j.neuropharm.2009.08.011.

Ströhle, A. et al. 'Reward anticipation and outcomes in adult males with attention-deficit/hyperactivity disorder.' *NeuroImage* 39; 3 (2008): 966–72. DOI:10.1016/j.neuroimage.2007.09.044.

Swanson, J. et al. 'Genes and attention-deficit hyperactivity disorder.' *Clinical Neuroscience Research* 1; 3 (2001): 207–16. DOI:10.1016/S1566-2772(01)00007-X.

Swanson, J.M. et al. 'Etiologic subtypes of attention-deficit/hyperactivity disorder: brain imaging, molecular genetic and environmental factors and the dopamine hypothesis.' *Neuropsychology Review* 17; 1 (2007): 39–59. DOI: 10.1007/s11065-007-9019-9.

Volkov, N.D. et al. 'Evaluating dopamine reward pathway in ADHD.' *Journal of the American Medical Association* 302; 10 (2009): 1084–91. DOI:10.1001/jama.2009.1308.

3. Natural Wanderers

Chen, C. et al. 'Population migration and the variation of dopamine D4 receptor (DRD4) allele frequencies around the globe.' *Evolution and Human Behavior* 20; 5 (1999): 309–24. DOI:10.1016/S1090-5138(99)00015-X.

Dein, S. 'Hunters in a farmer's world: ADHD and hunter gatherers.' *Anthropology* 3; 1 (2015). DOI:10.4172/2332-0915.1000150.

Ding, Y-C. et al. 'Evidence of positive selection acting at the human dopamine receptor D4 gene locus.' *PNAS* 99; 1 (2002): 309–14. DOI:10.1073/pnas.012464099.

Dobbs, D. 'Restless Genes.' *National Geographic*, Jan 2013.

Dreber, A. et al. 'The 7R polymorphism in the dopamine receptor D4 gene (DRD4) is associated with financial risk taking in men.' *Evolution and Human Behavior* 30; 2 (2009): 85–92. DOI:10.1016/j.evolhumbehav.2008.11.001.

Eisenberg, D.T.A. et al. 'Dopamine receptor genetic polymorphisms and body composition in undernourished pastoralists: an exploration of nutrition indices among nomadic and recently settled Ariaal men of northern Kenya.' *BMC Evolutionary Biology* 8; 173 (2008). DOI:10.1186/1471-2148-8-173.

Leung, P.W., et al. 'Family-based association study of DRD4 gene in methylphenidate-responded attention deficit/hyperactivity disorder.' *PLoS One* 12; 3 (2017): e0173748. DOI:10.1371/journal.pone.0173748.

Li, Z. et al. 'Molecular genetic studies of ADHD and its candidate genes: a review.' *Psychiatry Research* 219; 1 (2014): 10–24. DOI:10.1016/j.psychres.2014.05.005.

Moffitt, T. and Melchior, M. 'Why does the worldwide prevalence of childhood attention deficit hyperactivity disorder matter?' *American Journal of Psychiatry* 146; 6 (2007): 856–8. DOI:10.1176/appi.ajp.164.6.856.

Munafò, M. et al. 'Association of the dopamine D4 receptor (DRD4) gene and approach-related personality traits: meta-analysis and new data.' *Biological Psychiatry* 63; 2 (2008): 197–206. DOI:10.1016/j.biopsych.2007.04.006.

Oh, S-Y. and Kim, Y-K. 'Association of norepinephrine transporter gene poly-morphisms in attention-deficit/hyperactivity disorder in Korean population.' *Progress in Neuro-Psychopharmacology and Biological Psychiatry* S0278-5846; 16 (2016): 30326–8. DOI:10.1016/j.pnpbp.2016.10.006.

Polanczyk, G. et al. 'The worldwide prevalence of ADHD: a systematic review and metaregression analysis.' *American Journal of Psychiatry* 164; 6 (2007): 942–8. DOI:10.1176/ajp.2007.164.6.942.

Stringer, C. *The Origin of Our Species* (London, Penguin Books, 2011).

Stringer, C. *Lone Survivors: How We Came to Be the Only Humans on Earth* (New York, Henry Holt and Co., 2012).

4. An Engine for Curiosity

van Dongen, W.F.D. et al. 'Variation at the DRD4 locus is associated with wari-ness and local site selection in urban black swans.' *BMC Evolutionary Biology* 15; 253 (2015). DOI:10.1186/s12862-015-0533-8.

Ebstein, R.P. et al. 'Association between the dopamine D4 receptor gene exon III variable number of tandem repeats and political attitudes in female Han Chinese.' *Proceedings of the Royal Society B* 282; 1813 (2015). DOI:10.1098/rspb.2015.1360.

Settle, J.E. et al. 'Friendships moderate an association between a dopamine gene variant and political ideology.' *Journal of Politics* 72; 4 (2010): 1189–98. DOI:10.1017/S0022381610000617.

Wan, M. et al. 'DRD4 and TH gene polymorphisms are associated with activity, impulsivity and inattention in Siberian Husky dogs.' *Animal Genetics* 44; 6 (2013): 717–27. DOI:10.1111/age.12058.

5. Creative Daydreamers

Abraham, A. et al. 'Creative thinking in adolescents with attention deficit hyper-activity disorder (ADHD).' *Child Neuropsychology* 12; 2 (2006): 111–23. DOI:10.1080/09297040500320691.

Andrews-Hanna, J.R. et al. 'Evidence for the default network's role in spontan-eous cognition.' *Journal of Neurophysiology* 104; 1 (2010): 322 –35. DOI: 10.1152/jn.00830.2009.

Bashwiner, D.M. et al. 'Musical creativity "revealed" in brain structure: interplay between motor, default mode and limbic networks.' *Scientific Reports* 6; 20482 (2016). DOI:10.1038/srep20482.

Beaty, R.E. et al. 'Creativity and the default network: a functional connectivity analysis of the creative brain at rest.' *Neuropsychologia* 64 (2014): 92–8. DOI: 10.1016/j.neuropsychologia.2014.09.019.

Buckner, R.L. et al. 'The brain's default network: anatomy, function, and relevance to disease.' *Annals of the New York Academy of Sciences* 1124 (2008): 1–38. DOI:10.1196/annals.1440.011.

Carson, S.H. et al. 'Decreased latent inhibition is associated with increased creative achievement in high-functioning individuals.' *Journal of Personality and Social Psychology* 85; 3 (2003): 499–506. DOI:10.1037/0022-3514.85.3.499.

Farah, M.J. et al. 'When we enhance cognition with Adderall, do we sacrifice creativity? A preliminary study.' *Psychopharmacology* 202; 1–3 (2009): 541–7. DOI:10.1007/s00213-008-1369-3.

Healy, D. and Rucklidge, J.J. 'An investigation into the relationship among ADHD symptomatology, creativity, and neuropsychological functioning in children.' *Child Neuropsychology* 12; 6 (2006): 421–38. DOI:10.1080/09297040600806086.

Mohan, A. et al. 'The significance of the default mode network (DMN) in neurological and neuropsychiatric disorders: a review.' *Yale Journal of Biology and Medicine* 89; 1 (2016): 49–57. PMID: 27505016.

Smith, S.M. et al. 'Constraining effects of examples in a creative generation task.' *Memory and Cognition* 21; 6 (1993): 837–45. DOI:10.3758/bf03202751.

Sun, L. et al. 'Abnormal functional connectivity between the anterior cingulate and the default mode network in drug-naïve boys with attention deficit hyperactivity disorder.' *Psychiatry Research* 201; 2 (1012): 120–7. DOI:10.1016/j.pscychresns.2011.07.001.

Swartwood, M.O. et al. 'Stimulant treatment of ADHD: effects on creativity and flexibility in problem solving.' *Creativity Research Journal* 15; 4 (2003): 417–19. DOI:10.1207/S15326934CRJ1504_9.

Wells, M.F. et al. 'Thalamic reticular impairment underlies attention deficit in Ptchd1(Y/-) mice', *Nature* 532; 7597 (2016): 58–63. DOI:10.1038/nature17427.

White, H. et al. 'Thinking outside the box: Unconstrained creative generation in adults with attention deficit hyperactivity disorder.' *Journal of Creative Behavior* 54; 2 (2018):472–83.

White, H.A. and Shah, P. 'Uninhibited imaginations: creativity in adults with attention-deficit/hyperactivity disorder.' *Personality and Individual Differences* 40; 6 (2006): 1121–31. DOI:10.1016/j.paid.2005.11.007.

Zentall, S.S. et al. 'Social behavior in cooperative groups: students at risk for ADHD and their peers.' *Journal of Educational Research* 104; 1 (2011): 28–41. DOI:10.1080/00220670903567356.

6. Utterly Engrossed – Hyperfocus

Glickman, M.M. and Dodd, D.K. 'GUTI: a measure of urgent task involvement among adults with attention-deficit hyperactivity disorder.' *Psychological Reports* 82; 2 (1998): 592–4. DOI:10.2466/pr0.1998.82.2.592.

Palmitter, R.D. 'Dopamine signaling in the dorsal striatum is essential for motivated behaviors: lessons from dopamine-deficient mice.' *Annals of the New York Academy of Sciences* 1129 (2008): 35–46. DOI:10.1196/annals.1417.003.

Salamone, J.D. and Correa, M. 'The mysterious motivational functions of mesolimbic dopamine.' *Neuron* 76:3 (2012): 470–85. DOI:10.1016 /j.neuron. 2012.10.021.

7. Shattering Boundaries – Entrepreneurship

Mäntylä, T. et al. 'Decision making in adults with ADHD.' *Journal of Attention Disorders* 16; 2 (2012): 164–73. DOI:10.1177/1087054709360494.

Nicolaou, N. et al. 'A polymorphism associated with entrepreneurship: evidence from dopamine receptor candidate genes.' *Small Business Economics* 36 (2011): 151–5. DOI:10.1007/s11187-010-9308-1.

Nicolaou, N. et al. 'The influence of sensation seeking in the heritability of entrepreneurship.' *Strategic Entrepreneurship Journal* 2; 1 (2008): 7–21. DOI: 10.1002/sej.37.

Verheul, I. et al. 'The association between attention-deficit/hyperactivity (ADHD) symptoms and self-employment.' *European Journal of Epidemiology* 31; 8 (2016): 793–801. DOI:10.1007/s10654-016-0159-1.

Wiklund, J. et al. 'Entrepreneurship and psychological disorders: How ADHD can be productively harnessed.' *Journal of Business Venturing Insights* Vol 6 (2016): 14–20.

8. A Natural Remedy for ADHD – Movement

Baek, D-J. et al. 'Effect of treadmill exercise on social interaction and tyrosine hydroxylase expression in the attention-deficit/hyperactivity disorder rats.' *Journal of Exercise Rehabilitation* 10; 5 (2014): 252–7. DOI:10.12965/jer.140162.

Bubl, E. et al. 'Elevated background noise in adult attention deficit hyperactivity disorder is associated with inattention.' *PLoS One* 10; 2 (2015): e0118271. DOI:10.1371/journal.pone.011 8271.

Chang, Y-K. et al. 'Effect of acute exercise on executive function in children with attention deficit hyperactivity disorder.' *Archives of Clinical Neuropsychology* 27; 2 (2012): 225–37. DOI:10.1093/arclin/acr094.

Durston, S. et al. 'Magnetic resonance imaging of boys with attention-deficit/hyperactivity disorder and their unaffected siblings.' *Journal of the American Academy of Child & Adolescent Psychiatry* 43; 3 (2004): 332–40. DOI:10.1097/00004583-200403000-00016.

Gapin, J.I. et al. 'The effects of physical activity on attention deficit hyperactivity disorder symptoms: the evidence.' *Preventive Medicine* 52; 1 (2011): S70–4. DOI:10.1016/j.ypmed.2011.01.022.

Hoza, B. et al. 'A randomized trial examining the effects of aerobic physical activity on attention-deficit/hyperactivity disorder symptoms in young children.' *Journal of Abnormal Child Psychology* 43; 4 (2015): 655–67. DOI: 10.1007/s10802-014-9929-y.

Hoza, B. et al. 'Using physical activity to manage ADHD symptoms: the state of the evidence.' *Current Psychiatry Reports* 18; 12 (2016): 113. DOI:10.1007/s11920-016-0749-3.

Ma, J.K. et al. 'Four minutes of in-class high-intensity interval activity improves selective attention in 9-to-11-year olds.' *Applied Physiology Nutrition and Metabolism* 40; 3 (2015): 238–44. DOI:10.113 9/apnm-2014-0309.

McMorris, T. et al. 'Acute, intermediate intensity exercise, and speed and accuracy in working memory tasks: a meta-analytical comparison of effects.' *Physiology & Behavior* 102; 3–4 (2011): 421–8. DOI:10.1016/j.physbeh.2010.12.007.

Piepmeier, A.T. et al. 'The effect of acute exercise on cognitive performance in children with and without ADHD.' *Journal of Sport and Health Science* 4; 1 (2015): 97–104. DOI:10.1016/j.jshs.2014.11.004.

Rommel, A-S. et al. 'Is physical activity causally associated with symptoms of attention-deficit/hyperactivity disorder?' *Journal of the American Academy of Child & Adolescent Psychiatry* 54; 7 (2015): 565–70. DOI:10.1016/j.jaac.2015.04.011.

Salla, J. et al. 'ADHD symptomatology and perceived stress among French college students.' *Journal of Attention Disorders* 23; 14 (2019): 1711–18. DOI: 10.1177/1087054716685841.

Silva, A.P. et al, 'Measurement of the effect of physical exercise on the concentration of individuals with ADHD.' *PLoS One* 10; 3 (2015): e0122119. DOI: 10.1371/journal.pone.0122119.

Volkow, N.D. et al. 'Caffeine increases striatal dopamine D2/D3 receptor availability in the human brain.' *Translational Psychiatry* 5; 4 (2015): e549. DOI: 10.1038/tp.2015.46.

Wikipedia contributors. 'Terry Bradshaw.' *Wikipedia, the Free Encyclopedia*, <https://en.wikipedia.org/w/index.php?title=Terry_Bradshaw&oldid=1177973875> (accessed 4 Oct. 2023).

Ziereis, S. and Jansen, P. 'Effects of physical activity on executive function and motor performance in children with ADHD.' *Research in Developmental Disabilities* 38 (2015): 181–91. DOI:10.1016/j.ridd.2014.12.005.

9. School – A New Invention

Crichton, A. 'An inquiry into the nature and origin of mental derangement: comprehending a concise system of the physiology and pathology of the human mind and a history of the passions and their effects.' (1798) Printed for T. Cardell, Junior and W. Davies, in the strand.

Del Campo, N. et al. 'The roles of dopamine and noradrenaline in the pathophysiology and treatment of attention-deficit/hyperactivity disorder.' *Biological psychiatry* 69; 12 (2011): 145–57. DOI:10.1016/j.biopsych.2011.02.036.

Silva, A. et al. 'Measurement of the effect of physical exercise on the concentration of individuals with ADHD.' *PLoS One* 10: 3 (2015). e0122119.

Sveriges Television/Swedish Television. Nobelstudion. SVT2. Dec 7. 2016.

10. The Epidemic of Our Time

Del Campo, N. et al. 'The roles of dopamine and noradrenaline in the pathophysiology and treatment of attention-deficit/hyperactivity disorder.' *Biological Psychiatry* 69; 12 (2011): 145–57. DOI:10.1016/j.biopsych.2011.02.036.

Lo, M-T. et al. 'Genome-wide analyses for personality traits identify six genomic loci and show correlations with psychiatric disorders.' *Nature Genetics* 49; 1 (2017): 152–6. DOI:10.1038/ng.3736.

Pinker, S. *The Blank Slate: The Modern Denial of Human Nature* (London, Penguin Books, 2003).

Schwartz, A. *ADHD Nation: The Disorder, the Drugs, the Inside Story* (London, Little, Brown, 2016).

Silberman, S. *NeuroTribes: The Legacy of Autism and the Future of Neurodiversity* (New York, Avery, 2015).

Visser, S.N. et al. 'Trends in the parent-report of health care provider-diagnosed and medicated attention-deficit/hyperactivity disorder: United States 2003–2011.' *Journal of the American Academy of Child & Adolescent Psychiatry* 53; 1 (2014): 34–46. DOI:10.1016/j.jaac.2013.09.001.

de Zwaan, M. et al. 'The estimated prevalence and correlates of adult ADHD in a German community sample.' *European Archives of Psychiatry and Clinical Neuroscience* 262; 1 (2012): 79–86. DOI:10.1007/s00406-011-0211-9.

ACKNOWLEDGEMENTS

Thank you to my brother, Björn Hansen, who provided much valuable input and possesses a unique ability to instantly identify what is missing from a text or an argument. A big thank you also to Carl Johan Sundberg for bouncing ideas around, encouraging me to write the book and, as always, providing crystal-clear feedback. Thank you to my mother, Vanja Hansen, for all the encouragement and support, and to my father, Hans-Åke Hansen (1940–2011), who taught me to appreciate science.

A huge thank you to Martin Lorentzon for sharing your story.

The following people have contributed in various ways by brainstorming ideas, providing inspiration or making suggestions: Mats Thoren, Otto Ankarcrona, Karl Tobieson, Erik Telander, Mattias Ohlsson, Simon Kyaga, Minna Tunberger, Jonas Pettersson, Kristoffer Ahlbom, Tahir Jamil, Daniel Ek, Martin Sandqvist, Carl Johan Grandinson, Jenny Fuxe, Malou von Sivers, André Heinz and Anders Berntsson.

At my Swedish publisher, Bonnier Fakta, I would like to extend a big thank you to my publisher, Cecilia Viklund, and my editor,

Anna Paljak. You have been great as a sounding board and in helping to polish the manuscript – now I know the *delete* key exists for a reason. Thanks also to Eva Persson and Sofia Heurlin, who always do such a fantastic job with book launches and media contacts. A big thank you to Lisa Zachrisson, whose illustrations brought the text to life and transformed my Word document into a physical book. And of course, to my agent, Ulla Joneby, and her colleagues at Bonnier Rights, who have done an incredible job getting my books translated into so many languages. Thanks also to photographer Stefan Tell for the photos.

Finally, I want to thank all the ADHD patients I have met in my work. Through your unique strengths and weaknesses, limitations and talents, you have all helped me realise that our view on today's most hotly debated diagnosis is far too one-sided. You were the ones who made me want to change that!

All the patients I have described in the book are real persons, though I have altered details in their stories to ensure that no one will be identified or feel exposed.

INDEX

Note: page numbers in *italics* refer to information contained in tables.

and hyperfocus 92
and impulse control 11
individual differences in 156–8
malleability of 153
nonlinear 61
and pattern detection 143–4
size 22–3, 155
see also default mode network;
  frontal lobe; nucleus accumbens;
  thalamus
brain imaging 155
brain injury 165
brainstorming 63–5, 77

caffeine 124–5
Cambridge University 97–8
cancer 49
cardiac health 147
cell division 49
chaos 23, 83, 150
chefs 89–90, 91, 92–3
Cheyenne tribe 38
children
  and ADHD diagnosis 10, 141–3,
    146, 148, 155–6, 158
  and ADHD medication 148
  benefits of movement for
    114–19, 127
  and brainstorming 64
  and concentration and movement
    114–19, 127
  and impulsivity and movement
    115, 116
  prevalence of ADHD amongst
    11, 141
  and task-solving in group settings
    77–8
  and video game performance 115–16

see also boys; girls
China *40*, 41, 98, 129
Chlorocebus monkey 56
chunking tasks 82, 94, 95, 137
climate change 39, 48, 49
cocaine 31, 32, 149
coffee 124–5, 126
concentration 79
  and ADHD medication 72
  anatomy of 123
  and caffeine 125
  and dopamine 29–31
  and focusing on one task at a
    time 110
  modern life's demands on 145–6
  and the nucleus accumbens 160
  under pressure 93
  see also hyperfocus
concentration difficulties 3, 7–9, 43,
    45–6, 72, 133, 155, 164
  in adults 11–12
  and attention deficit disorder 13
  causes of 12, 23, 123
  and dopamine 30–1
  and gender 10
  and hyperfocus 86
  and 'leaky attention' 68–70,
    75–6, 81
  and movement 111–14, 115–21,
    126–8, 136–7
  and the nucleus accumbens 17–20
  and social situations 90–1
  and understimulation 25
  and working memory training 138
  see also streams of thought
Conners, Keith 141
conscientiousness 153
conservatism 55

ABOUT THE AUTHOR

Dr Anders Hansen is a Swedish psychiatrist, speaker and international bestselling author with his own TV series exploring the human brain. Dr Hansen's books have sold millions of copies globally and topped bestseller lists around the world. He is the winner of the book of the year Big Health Award 2017 and 2019, and Sweden's Mensa Prize 2018.

Dr Hansen is also the author of *The Happiness Cure*, *The Attention Fix* and *The Mind-Body Method*.

Also by Dr Anders Hansen

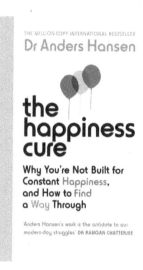

The Happiness Cure

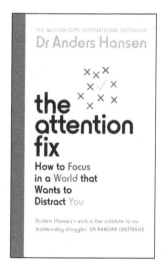

The Attention Fix

The Mind-Body Method